How Healthy Intimac͏ d

Better
Than
WINE

Steven R. Saindon

Better Than Wine:
How Healthy Intimacy in Marriage Reveals God
Copyright © 2021 by Steven R. Saindon

Unless otherwise indicated, all Scripture references are from the *Holy Bible, New International Version,* copyright ©1973, 1978, 1984, 2011 by Biblica, Inc. Used by permission. All rights reserved worldwide.

Cover design by Roy Appalsamy of Toronto, Canada. Interior layout by Toney Mulhollan. Copy editing by Amy Morgan.

Illumination Publishers titles may be purchased in bulk for classroom instruction, teaching seminars, or sales promotional use. For information, please email paul.ipibooks@me.com.

Illumination Publishers cares deeply about using renewable resources and uses recycled paper whenever possible.

Steve and Kelli Saindon have been married for over 35 years and have served in the ministry that entire time. They have led ministries in Chicago, St. Louis, Vancouver, Toronto, Detroit, Los Angeles and Minneapolis-St. Paul. In addition, they have three happily married adult children and four rambunctious grandchildren. In recent years they have enjoyed helping couples grow in their marriage relationship and become stronger in the Lord. Steve is currently the evangelist of the Racine Church of Christ in Wisconsin and is currently working on his second book! For more information about his ministry go to his website at www.N2FM.org.

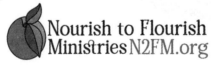

Nourish to Flourish Ministries N2FM.org

ILLUMINATION **ip**
PUBLISHERS

www.ipibooks.com

I eagerly dedicate
this book to my bride.
Kelli,
I cannot put into words how
much I adore you.
You are my
greatest gift from God.

CONTENTS

CONTENTS

Acknowledgements

Dad and Mom, your faithful love for each other is the main reason I am so passionate about marriage.

Michael Burns, you were the first to help me believe I could write a book.

Joel Nagel, you were my most consistent encourager in the six years it took me to finish this book.

Tomm Wilson, you got me through the toughest time in my life, so that I was even capable of writing a book.

Leanne Bishop, thank you for your support in the early stages of this endeavor.

Dear family (Dustin, Stevi, Kaleb, Kaylin, Kyle, and Sadie), your support for me and love for each other is amazing.

Joel and Christy Peed, Rick and Heather Mekemson, and Calvin and Elaine Johnson, your marriages inspire me.

Dustin Young, Lisa Payne, and Mike Saindon, your enthusiasm for this project kept me going when my own enthusiasm waned.

Minneapolis and Racine churches, you graciously allowed me to take time away from day-to-day ministry so I could write.

Marci Arneson and Tammy Fleming, I cannot put into words how much your wisdom and insights on chapters four, five, and six guided me.

Anita and Camille Cruise, thank you for working hard on the final edit, I am so grateful for your fine-tuning.

Shelley and Heidi, the two best baristas on the planet, marriage is better than wine and only slightly better than your coffee.

Stevi Wood, this book wouldn't even exist if it were not for all your editing and advice [EDIT: You're welcome!].

And Kelli, no one has taught me more about love than you have.

Introduction

Dear Seekers,

What do candlelight, flirtatious glances, racing hearts, moans, sighs, naked laughter, and entangled bodies have to do with God? If you are not married, nothing! Well, the candlelight is fine if you are in a crowded restaurant. Everything else on that passionate little list belongs in marriage. The Bible teaches that these breathtaking moments have everything to do with God. They reveal to us big and important things about our Creator. As history, mountains, animal life, and galaxies (Psalms 19:1–6) preach powerful "sermons" about God, so does romance. Theologian Christopher West has this to say about the deeper meanings of bedroom love:

> Sexual love is the earthly key that enables us to enter into heaven's song. How often does Scripture invite us to "break into song" or to "sing a new song"? What song do you think Scripture is inviting us to sing if not the greatest of all songs, the Song of Songs? As saints throughout history attest, this erotic song provides the "mystical key" that opens the "holy door" to deep union and intimacy with God. For, as Scripture teaches, the one-flesh union is a great mystery that refers to Christ and his union with the church (Ephesians 5:31–32).[1]

He also writes:

> Odd as it may seem to some, a proper vision of our sexuality (the fruit of integration) provides the clearest window for catching a glimpse of the "great mystery" of God's ultimate plan for our lives and the universe. Conversely, a distorted vision of our sexuality serves as one of the most effective blocks to understanding who God really is, who we really are, and what the "great mystery" of Christianity is really all about. No wonder the enemy so viciously attacks

our sexuality!

Lucifer is the great plagiarizer. He takes what belongs to Christ and puts his own name on it, claiming the erotic realm for himself. Tragically, it seems that many Christians are content to let him have it. It is not uncommon to encounter people who—in the name of supposed "piety"—find the very idea of linking erotic love and Christ's love unconscionable. In adopting this attitude, however, we do not overcome the deceiver's lies; we unwittingly buy into them. We must not surrender the erotic realm to the enemy! We must not let his distortions bind us to our own lusts and blind us to the "great mystery" revealed through our bodies! Precarious as it is, we must be courageous in reclaiming the erotic sphere for Christ and his church. For, as both Old and New Testaments teach us—and as we see especially in the Song of Songs—the erotic sphere is the privileged realm of a divine revelation.

Reclaiming the erotic sphere for Christ does not mean, of course, that we bring eros back "as is" from the enemy's turf. Rightly do the pious recoil at this idea. For appealing to the lustful distortions of our sexuality as images of the divine would be blasphemy. Rather, in the process of reclaiming the erotic realm for Christ, we must submit all that is "erotic" to a radical transformation.[2]

Such a radical transformation must be carefully guided by Scripture (1 Timothy 4:1–8; 2 Timothy 2:15). We dare not guess, follow our feelings, or be swept up in current cultural definitions about things that unveil profound and holy mysteries about God. Marriage and sex are a sacred gift from God tasked with the divine assignment to draw us into our immense, yet intimate, Creator, a God who is always filled with inexpressible joy. A God who is far different from the anemic caricatures that many of us grew up with.

I can be relentless in my Bible study. In the last forty-one years as a Christian, I have studied many topics to get to know our amazing God. What I have penned in this little book has changed my life far more than anything I've ever studied. I sincerely hope it will be a blessing for you also. Here is a summary of each chapter so you have an idea of where we are going.

Chapter 1: SHAME(LESS)

Jesus, who was a fulfillment of many Old Testament prophecies, came to restore the intimate joy between God and us—this is why the first picture of the kingdom was a wedding in Cana (John 2).

Chapter 2: MYSTERY

A healthy Christian marriage reveals profound mysteries about our relationship with God, both now and in the future. The Holy Spirit works especially through the wisdom literature of the Bible to show us how to be prophetic lovers.

Chapter 3: IMAGE

Among other things, we were created to image the intimate love between Father, Son, and Holy Spirit. Whether married or single, this is the most fundamental purpose of human beings.

Chapter 4: ROLES

From the beginning, God designed the two genders with specific roles and responsibilities similar to the different roles that exist within the Godhead. Failure to embrace these responsibilities has a negative impact on God-honoring intimacy.

Chapter 5: HUSBANDS

How a husband can be a place of security and intoxicating joy for his bride, so as to be effective in unveiling his part of the profound mystery of marriage— demonstrating Christ's love for his bride.

Chapter 6: WIVES
How a wife can be a place of strength and intoxicating joy for her husband, so as to be effective in unveiling her part of the profound mystery of marriage—demonstrating how the bride of Christ eagerly surrenders herself to her Bridegroom.

Chapter 7: INTOXICATION
The occasional moments of unbridled joy in connecting with your earthly spouse will give way to an infinite intoxication with our eternal Husband.

Dear Sisters,

I hope you find this book to be a blessing to you. My desire is that you experience much inspiration from God in pursuing further what he has created you to be. Chapter six, "Wives," was for me the most difficult to write (stating the obvious) because I'm not a woman. It is medically proven that my brain is radically different from my wife's brain. So regardless of how hard I try, my perspective is that of a man. Although I have grown in this area, I know I tend to be insensitive. In this book we will venture to discuss the most intimate areas of life. I have worked to do this with as much care and thoughtfulness as I can. The last thing I want to do is to discourage, overwhelm, or crush anyone. In the process of writing, I tapped the shoulders of several women whom I respect greatly, so that the final product would be inspiring. Some of these women I know very well, others only by reputation. I am extremely grateful for their encouragement, wisdom, and insights. Furthermore, in the last few years approximately 90 percent of the books that I have read were authored by women theologians. I am trying with all my might to understand the beautiful woman God gave to me, and as a minister, I want to be as effective as possible with the female half of my congregation. So, my dear sisters, I hope that you don't find anything that I've written to be insensitive in any way. Being inspirational, challenging, and at the same time aware of every perspective is not something many are good at. Thankfully, it is something our Lord excelled at. It is one of the many reasons he was so effective while ministering to women. I ask you to give me grace and the benefit of the doubt, and I hope my clumsiness in this area will not be a distraction as you read.

It is much easier to accept a challenge from God if you are convinced that you are already deeply valued, that he already adores you. It is difficult to put into words the high view that God has of women. Throughout history there have been more than a few sloppy theologians who have claimed the Bible is down on women. But this is simply not true. According to the Bible, women are an influential and powerful creation. And that power can be wielded either positively or negatively. Proverbs ends with the picture of a virtuous woman that a man should pursue. This piece of poetry, often underappreciated by men, is God's opinion of the beauty, value, strength, and power of a godly woman. In speaking of the Proverbs 31 woman, theologian Ellen Davis says this:

> *Although the topic of good and bad women is common in Egyptian and Babylonian wisdom instructions, nothing in all ancient Near Eastern literature matches this tribute to a woman's strength, dignity and social power. Moreover, within Hebrew scripture this is the most unambiguously flattering portrait of any individual, man or woman.*[3]

Abraham married one of the greatest, though one of the most underrated, heroes in the Bible, and Sarah was one of the reasons he became the father of our faith (1 Peter 3:1–6; Genesis 12, 20). How often have we heard a man stand behind a podium

and say, "If it hadn't been for my mother..." or "If it weren't for my amazing wife, I would have never accomplished these things"?

In the book of Proverbs, wisdom is personified as a beautiful woman.

> Does not wisdom call out?
>> Does not understanding raise HER voice?
> At the highest point along the way,
>> where the paths meet, SHE takes HER stand.
> (Proverbs 8:1–2, emphasis mine)

> Wisdom has built HER house;
>> SHE has set up its seven pillars.
> SHE has prepared HER meat and mixed HER wine;
>> SHE has also set HER table.
> (Proverbs 9:1–2, emphasis mine)

> The beginning of wisdom is this: Get wisdom.
>> Though it cost all you have, get understanding.
> Cherish HER and SHE will exalt you;
>> embrace HER and SHE will honor you.
> (Proverbs 4:7–8, emphasis mine)

> SHE speaks with wisdom,
>> and faithful instruction is on HER tongue.
> (Proverbs 31:26, emphasis mine)

The Proverbs father is challenging his son to pursue wisdom as he would a woman that he is crazy about. What if we had a whole generation of young men who ran after wisdom the way they run after women? What would happen to a community of young men "infatuated" with God's instruction? What would they become? Wisdom is also personified as a woman because without women's insights we could never know God as deeply as we should.

Mary of Bethany is one of my favorite theologians. Because she was wired by her Creator so differently from a man, she understood things about Jesus that even his best friends (men) did not comprehend. Her uncommon understanding of Jesus and her extravagant response is something Jesus wants referred to anytime and anywhere the gospel is preached. How did this peasant woman pick up things about Jesus that his closest friends completely missed, even though they spent so much more time with him than she did? Men, husbands, to know our God deeply, we desperately need the women and wives that God has surrounded us with. No one has taught me more about God and his love than the wife that he has gifted to me. And now I am watching my daughters who have become wives and mothers, and I'm learning even more. I love conversing with them about the deeper things of life because they always bring a unique and godly perspective. Sometimes our conversations can even get a bit "spicy." But they always end with love, laughter, and growth. Men, married or single, we will never understand certain facets of God without giving great respect to the women that he has blessed us with.

The very first woman, Eve, was the last brushstroke painted on the canvas of creation. In a sense, she was the crescendo of the creation song. It was after she was expertly crafted by God that he said of his creation that it was "very good." She was created to be emotionally, intellectually, and physically different from Adam so that together they might know and represent God more fully. Furthermore, if you check the record (Genesis 2:7, 19, 21–22), she was created differently from any other living creature. Every living being, male or female, was made from clay. But she was made from something incredibly special, a part of Adam himself. Her unique creation must mean something big— which I am still pondering on and trying to figure out. Without her, Adam could have never begun to image (our purpose) the Divine Family we know as God. He would have no way to fill the earth (our mission) with more and more image bearers. Eve was the very first Queen of Creation (Song of Songs 6:8–10).

So, my dear sisters, I write this to let you know that I have the highest respect for women. And any challenge in this book that is delivered in your direction is meant to inspire you to reach your full potential as the *most beautiful part* of God's creation.

Dear Singles,

Even though this is a book about marriage, my aim is to also instruct and encourage singles. The first reason is pretty obvious: someday you may find that special someone and get married. I wish that thirty-five years ago, when I married my wife, I had had the benefit of at least some of the biblical wisdom I do now. Another reason that I encourage singles to read this book is because it's about not only human marriage, but also our marriage to God. Ten years ago when I began my relentless study of marriage, I had no idea how much it would benefit my intimacy with God. So even if you never get married in this life, I believe there are many pictures and principles within this book that will help you draw near to God. I tried my absolute best to write unashamedly about marriage and sex without this book needing an "R rating."

I took my cues from the *Song of Songs*, which is deeply passionate, yet never vulgar. There's not a "padlock" on the most sensual book of the Bible, so I didn't want one on this book either. In ancient Israel, the *Song of Songs* was sung at every wedding and even during the Passover. Everyone knew this highly instructive book of relational wisdom.

My dear single brothers and sisters, marriage is a valuable thing in the eyes of God. However, and this is especially important to understand, singles should never be looked at as second-class citizens of the kingdom of God. The New Testament does not teach that it is better to be married. It actually teaches that there are huge advantages to being a single disciple and that in some cases it is the better choice (1 Corinthians 7). Some of the people I respect the most in the world are people who have decided to skip the temporary symbol of human marriage and passionately, like the Apostle Paul, go after the reality—Jesus Christ our Bridegroom.

One last note—spiritual and relational intoxication is a big theme in this book. That's why the book is entitled *Better Than Wine*. However, I do not want to be misunderstood in any way: I firmly believe and obey what the Bible teaches, that drunkenness from alcohol or any like substance is a sin (Galatians 5:21).

CHAPTER 1

Shame(less)

When the Son of God stepped down from his throne to become a man, the finest of heaven's wines funneled itself into the common earthen vessel of a Palestinian Jew. For thirty years this vintage from heaven was cellared away in a carpenter's shop in Nazareth. But now the time has come for the seal to be broken, the cork extracted, and the fragrant bouquet of deity to fill the earth so that, for a fleeting but festive moment, <u>the world's parched lips might taste the kingdom of God</u>, that time coincided, appropriately, with a wedding.[4] (emphasis mine)

Your love is better than wine. (Song of Songs 1:2 ESV)

Picture this: God rests above the face of the deep; the earth is formless and void. With just a word, light bursts forth. With more words he first separates light and darkness, then land and sea, then the sky from the earth. And then he fills it all with vegetation, birds of the air, fish for the sea, and every kind of animal conceivable to inhabit the earth. It is lush and beautiful, a place of worship.

By the breath of God, man is created and given stewardship of God's new temple. Everything seems balanced, yet something—or better said, someone—is missing. So from the man's own body God forms woman, making them wholly separate yet wholly one flesh. Their creation and their union are the pinnacle of all creation. The world begins with a wedding.

Now picture this: it is the third day of the wedding celebration in Cana of Galilee. Already there have been two nights of joyous fellowship. Family and friends have gathered each evening to lay aside their work and rejoice with the new couple. The third night of festivities has already started; music and the smell of cooking food fills the air. Fires are lit and stoked to give the partygoers light, and the community chorus is singing Solomon's *Song of Songs*. Though most are not aware, the exquisite wine they lift to their lips is the first miracle performed by a rabbi. The restoration of God's new world begins with a wedding.

Adam and Eve began their marriage together in a most breathtaking way. They were lovingly placed by their Creator in the garden of holy pleasure ("Eden" means pleasure). In this sacred garden they enjoyed unhindered fellowship with each other and their King. They could look into the holy face of God without even the slightest insecurity. There was no sin in this blissful place, only the possibility of it. And since there was no sin, there was no shame, the ugliest of all emotions. Truly, they were "naked and unashamed." They were fully known by each other and God, and get this, they *wanted* to be fully known. Adam and Eve wanted to reveal everything about themselves to everyone, because they felt so good about themselves. Can you imagine never feeling any shame about anything? What would it feel like to do an intense examination of everything about yourself, and all you find is pure and beautiful...a spiritual super-model inside and out. Your intimacy with God and everyone else would have no obstacles, and your joy would be inexpressible. Adam and Eve radiated perfect confidence without the slightest arrogance. For them, intimacy on every level and of every kind was easy, even natural. They not only loved each other with the purest love, they also loved themselves that way. This kind of holy, shame-free atmosphere had an intoxicating effect on the first couple. They experienced the full joy potential of every kind of intimacy: spiritual, intellectual, emotional, and sexual. The relational wine of God's love was flowing full strength through the middle of their heart and soul.

At that wedding in Cana, Jesus was showing through his first miracle that his ministry was all about restoring that shame-free, intimate love. God cannot stand the relational distance between us and him. The entire Bible is the story of our Creator who will not stop until he has completely recovered what he had with us at the beginning: an intimate relationship free of shame.

Weddings in the ancient Jewish world were much different from our marriage ceremonies today. The wedding recorded in John chapter two probably went something like this: After the bridegroom finished building the couple's new home, usually an addition to his parents' house, his father would inspect it. If everything met his expectations, the father would tell his son to go and fetch his bride. Sounds like the beginning of John 14, doesn't it?

> "Do not let your hearts be troubled. You believe in God; believe also in me. My Father's house has many rooms; if that were not so, would I have told you that I am going there to prepare a place for you? And if I go and prepare a place for you, I will come back and take you to be with me that you also may be where I am." (John 14:1–3)

The reason it sounds similar is because this is wedding language, and everyone knew it; but like us, at that time the apostles probably didn't catch the gravity of it. Jesus, our Bridegroom, is building us a home. At the right time, his Father is going to tell him to go fetch his bride. When the son received the green light, he, along with his groomsmen, would travel across town to initiate the ceremony. There would be a festive parade with the entire bridal party back to his newly built home. The priest would conduct the ceremony similarly to the way we do things today. However, after the couple were pronounced husband and wife, the celebration was orchestrated much differently. After the "I do's" the new husband would escort his bride into their home and consummate their marriage, while everyone waited outside to begin the celebration. Our Jewish forefathers were not ashamed or embarrassed about God's good gift of sex, as so many of us are today.

After the couple celebrated their oneness in a beautiful physical embrace, they would exit their honeymoon suite, not to go off by themselves to some tropical paradise, but rather to their friends and family. So for a week, or even two, they would all celebrate together. The whole community. During the day they would work their fields and shepherd their sheep. In the evening they would come together to celebrate with the bride and groom. Every night they would party...with a "G rating," of course. They would dance, and the community chorus would sing love songs, especially the greatest love song ever written, Solomon's *Song of Songs*. Everyone knew this mysterious song because it was sung at every wedding. Night after night the community would witness the lovesick couple, and for a brief time, everything felt good in the universe. Can you imagine how therapeutic this weeklong celebration would be for all the married people of the community? It was kind of like a honeymoon for everyone. This would help through the challenges and complexities of life to keep their marriages strong, vibrant, and passionate. We love weddings, but I have a feeling, not nearly as much as our Jewish forefathers did.

I've often wondered what Jesus talked about with his new disciples as they gathered night after night. After turning a whole bunch of water into wine, did he talk about the "new wine" prophecies? (Amos 9:13; Joel 3:18; Isaiah 25:6–8).

> Then the Lord will appear over them;
>> his arrow will flash like lightning.
> The Sovereign LORD will sound the trumpet;
>> he will march in the storms of the south,
>> and the LORD Almighty will shield them.
> They will destroy
>> and overcome with slingstones.
> They will drink and roar as with wine;
>> they will be full like a bowl

used for sprinkling the corners of the altar.
The LORD their God will save his people on that day
    as a shepherd saves his flock.
They will sparkle in his land
    like jewels in a crown.
How attractive and beautiful they will be!
    Grain will make the young men thrive,
    and new wine the young women. (Zechariah 9:14–17)

The Ephraimites will become like warriors,
    and their hearts will be glad as with wine.
Their children will see it and be joyful;
    their hearts will rejoice in the LORD. (Zechariah 10:7)

Zechariah 9:15 and 10:7 are pictures of God's new covenant people under the Messiah. The metaphor is powerful. "They," the people of the new covenant, will look like they are roaring drunk because of their King. The hearts of the future Ephraimites will be "glad as with wine." Their "children will see" their joy in the Lord and be attracted to the kingdom. That is what these two prophetic passages are teaching.

As he fellowshipped with Peter, James, John, and the other disciples, did Jesus point out the "relational drunkenness" of the happy couple as the first and best picture of his kingdom?

For the kingdom of God is not a matter of eating and drinking, but of righteousness, peace and joy in the Holy Spirit, because anyone who serves Christ in this way is pleasing to God and receives human approval. (Romans 14:17–18-9)

Jesus only had about 1000 days to turn the world upside down and begin the replanting of Eden (Revelation 21–22). Yet he spends an entire week at a wedding with his new disciples. Maybe Jesus looked at his future church builders and said something like this: "Listen, my friends, I am no ordinary rabbi. I am not some typical teacher. I am here, and you are here also, to restore Eden and to make this world a suitable place for the presence of God once again. My Father owns this messed up place, and he wants it all back. And he's going to get it all back. This will be a great struggle and we will suffer ominously; that's a promise! The serpent is not going to idly sit by as we replant what he ruined. Do you see that happy couple up there at the head table? The joy they are saturated with is but the tiniest reflection of the eternal joy that awaits the lovers of God. Do you hear those lyrics? Can you smell the aroma of extravagant love that fills this place? It's all just a hint, a mere shadow of the intoxicating joy that is going to overtake the bride forever (thinking of Isaiah 35:10). This world will be one joyous soul again."

I think Jesus wanted this picture of the kingdom deeply imprinted on their hearts. Discipleship can be drudgery if you do not have a clear picture of its glorious outcome. The "joy set before him" was one of the main reasons Jesus persevered with enthusiasm (Hebrews 12:1–4).

I've been a Christian now for a little over forty-one years. It's a little embarrassing to admit this, but most of those years were characterized by more drudgery than delight. I believe I gave my life to Christ from good motives. I was blown away when it finally hit me that God became a man and then was crucified for all the foolish and stupid things I've done. So I energetically committed myself to my new King. I was weary of being my own king. Yet for years as a committed, albeit imperfect follower, I experienced little joy. Certainly not the inexpressible and glorious kind (1 Peter 1:8–9). Plagued with an overactive, guilt-ridden, "I can never do enough" conscience, I wrestled with it every day. At church, even as an evangelist, I often wondered, *"Am I the only one who is not happy around here?"* Most of my peers thought that my wife and I were doing great as church leaders, because our churches usually grew. A few years ago the consistent grind in my relationship with God was wearing me down to the point of burnout. The frustration I felt spilled out into almost all my relationships, especially with my wife. About ten years ago a friend of mine made a pointed observation over lunch. He said, "Steve, I don't think you and your wife are very close." At first I felt defensive and threw out a few excuses. But then I caught myself, looked at my friend and said, "You know what, brother? You're right. I'm not close with my wife and haven't been for a long time." I thanked him profusely for his gentle honesty because I knew this was going to be one of those life-changing conversations that God had set up. It was at that moment that I realized I wasn't good at intimacy. My marriage to Kelli was just like my relationship with God. Devoted, but distant and frustrating. I also realized it was possible to be sold out for Jesus yet have an unhealthy relationship with him. Kelli and I are as willing as anyone to do whatever for God. I mean, we've moved over twenty times to help build the kingdom by planting and reviving churches. I tried hard to honor my vows to both Jesus and my bride, but the joy was missing, largely because I did not know how to intimately love. How could I as a minister lead the bride of Christ to a healthy place when my relationship with my own bride was not healthy? And how could I help the hundreds of people I was leading to thrive in their relationship with God, if I wasn't thriving? This all led me to a study of the wisdom literature in the Bible, especially the *Song of Songs*. The book you are reading is the fruit of that study and has radically changed my relationship with both God and my wife. Today I am deeply and joyously connected with both God and my bride. At least, most of the time.

Shame is the intensely painful feeling that we are unworthy of love. —Brené Brown

Shame was the first consequence of our sin, and it immediately ruined our relational drunkenness with God and each other. Shame is debilitating to any kind of intimacy. And shame is the chief reason why I struggled with being intimately close with God and Kelli for so many years. Enduring a lot of shame is not necessarily a sign of a bad heart, but it is a sign of either an immature or an unhealthy relationship with God.

My wife is one of those beautiful souls who never thinks she does enough, or is enough, for her God or me. Yet she is such a relentless and selfless servant. She is my Proverbs 31 woman. One of my most diligent prayers is that she (and the bride of Christ) would see how amazing she truly is. But shame has stunted her ability to see herself accurately, just as it has with me, and pretty much all of us. The bride of Christ, the church, would be much more effective if she saw herself the way Jesus does. I used to think that God didn't like me very much, that he pretty much just tolerated me. I think a lot of Christians feel that way, and I think it makes God sad. I know that to be true because I tell my wife all the time how amazing she is, yet she struggles to believe it, and that also makes me sad.

I am thankful for healthy guilt feelings. They stop me when I am headed in the wrong direction and prompt me to go the right way. But I see no redeeming value for shame of any kind. Guilt says I did something bad and ugly. Shame says I am bad and ugly. Some people have lived within an atmosphere of shame (self-loathing) for so long that they don't even know what it would feel like to breathe in good and gracious thoughts about themselves. The Bible says we are supposed to love ourselves, though not in a narcissistic or selfish way. Truth be known, a person cannot truly love others if they intensely dislike their own self.

The insecurity that shame causes will prompt us to hold back in our relationships with God and others. We will parcel ourselves out in acceptable bits and pieces. Joy-bringing intimacy is strangled by low self-esteem. And a low self-esteem is the fruit of a soul that has been conquered by shame. Our relationship with God, with our spouse, or with anyone else will not flourish amid shame. I know people who have many insecurities, yet they love God as much as anyone I know. I say that because many of those friends of mine are ashamed of their insecurities, and they think it's all because they do not love God.

All the way back in 1980 I had a little three-minute conversation with my campus minister that radically changed my life. It's very possible that I would have left God and the church if it were not for Andy Van Buren's timely words. I was just a few months old as a Christian, and my fragile faith was full of doubts and discouragement. The honeymoon with Jesus was definitely over for me, and I was depressed. Andy attentively listened to my "baby-blues story," and then he said something that I treasure to this very day: "Steve, you are a young Christian, so you're going to have many struggles in your faith. But one thing I know about you: you have a genuine heart and I know you love God." It wasn't just what he said that helped me so much, but rather how he said it. I could tell that he really believed that I loved God from my heart. And that was my biggest insecurity and worry. I still struggled with far too much shame for many years as I learned to roll over, crawl, and then walk as a Christian. In the toughest times, I hung on to Andy's words, believing for the most part that I really did love God. Yet for a long time I was a gut-it-out Christian. I remember thinking, *"Happiness is overrated. I don't need to be happy, I just need to be humble and get my Christian chores done."* Happiness is not the purpose of life as so many believe it is. However, it is a sign of a healthy relationship with God.

Our bridegroom King does not want only compliance, no matter how impressive it is. No, the ultimate reason he gave his life was to be intimately connected. He is dying (pun intended) to be crazy close to every one of us. Forgiven, yet not close— that's not enough for him. Saved at a distance—the King is not content with that. Devoted, but lacking deep intimacy—that's not what the Lord longs for. It seems to me that the King at the beginning (Genesis 2) and at the re-beginning (John 2) started things off with a wedding to reveal the deepest cravings of his big heart. He profoundly aches to be one with each of us in the most intimate ways possible. And the reason he is so passionate for us is because *he really is our bridegroom King.*

Within the pages of Scripture there are many parables, prophecies, poems, and pictures of who God is so that we can know him accurately and deeply. God is our Father, our Shepherd, our Creator, a consuming fire, a warrior, a refuge, a strong tower, our hiding place, the majestic glory, the "Holy, Holy, Holy One," and so much more. Each of these pictures of God gives us a little slice of who he really is. In my opinion, the most dominant metaphor of God in the Bible is the picture of him as our bridegroom King. I could write an entire chapter on why I believe that, but I will be succinct and just share a few reasons. First, the Bible opens and closes with a wedding ceremony, and Jesus kicks off the new creation at a wedding. Second, in John 3:29, John the Baptist, Jesus' cousin, introduces him as the Bridegroom. Third, the prophets so often talk about God as our spiritual husband that they could be referred to as marriage counselors (Hosea; Isaiah 54:5, 62:5; Jeremiah 2–3, 31; Ezekiel 16, 23). Fourth, God always looked at his covenant relationship with us as a marriage.

> The word of the LORD came to me: "Go and proclaim in the hearing of Jerusalem:
> "This is what the LORD says:
> "'I remember the devotion of your youth,
>   how as a bride you loved me
> and followed me through the wilderness,
>   through a land not sown.
> Israel was holy to the LORD,
>   the firstfruits of his harvest;
> all who devoured her were held guilty,
>   and disaster overtook them,'"
> declares the LORD. (Jeremiah 2:1–3)

This next passage is quite amazing:

"Is not Israel still my son,
my darling child?" says the LORD.
"I often have to punish him,
    but I still love him.
That's why I long for him
    and surely will have mercy on him.
Set up road signs;
    put up guideposts.
Mark well the path
    by which you came.
Come back again, my virgin Israel;
    return to your towns here.
How long will you wander,
    my wayward daughter?
For the LORD will cause something new to happen—
    Israel will embrace her God." (Jeremiah 31:20–22 NLT)

In this section of Jeremiah's message, he is preaching to the northern kingdom (Israel), which had been destroyed over 100 years earlier. The last prophet who was sent to Israel before Assyria bulldozed her into the ground was Hosea. Hosea was the brokenhearted bridegroom whose wife (Gomer) became a prostitute. His marriage became a picture of God's pain-filled marriage with Israel and God's last-ditch effort to save Israel from destruction. God was hoping that his broken heart would break their hearts and cause them to repent. The message to Israel was clear: in her marriage to God she had become a whoring ingrate. Yet many decades later, look what Jeremiah says to God's prostitute ex-wife. The prophet uses two metaphors to describe God's deep longings. First, God is described as a loving father who is still yearning for his son's return. Second, he is pictured as a husband who is still hoping for the return of his prostitute wife. After so many years, God is still wishing and hoping. What an amazing God we have! But get this: Jeremiah says that if the whore repents, God will look at her as a virgin. In other words, in his eyes it will be as if she never messed up. The Bridegroom is willing to draw a line in the sand and start completely over, as if nothing ever happened. Even after her decades of flagrant sinning, she can still be a shame-free spiritual virgin. Then Jeremiah says that God is going to do something so new, different, and unheard of that it will cause Israel the prostitute to finally "embrace her God." Through the cross, God will finally have the marriage with Israel, and us, that he always longed for: a shame-free, super-intimate marriage (see Hosea 2).

This is all-important because it makes a difference in how we view that mysterious book in the middle of the Bible called the *Song of Songs*. Ancient theologians, for the most part, looked at it as an allegory of God's relationship with Israel. Modern theologians view it mostly as a marriage and sex manual. Like Psalms 2, 22, and 45, it is one of those sections of Scripture that does double duty. The *Song of Songs* is definitely a book about marital intimacy. However, it is also a picture of our relationship with our bridegroom King, Jesus Christ. Studying this beautiful poetry has completely revamped how I view the way God sees me, sees us.

How beautiful you are, my darling!
Oh, how beautiful!
Your eyes are doves. (Song of Songs 1:15)

You are altogether beautiful, my darling;
there is no flaw in you. (Song of Songs 4:7)

You have stolen my heart, my sister, my bride;
you have stolen my heart
with one glance of your eyes,
with one jewel of your necklace.
How delightful is your love, my sister, my bride!
How much more pleasing is your love than wine,
and the fragrance of your perfume

more than any spice! (Song of Songs 4:9–10)

Throughout this passionate little book, the King cannot stop praising his bride for her beauty. Believe it or not, this is how Jesus views his redeemed people.

> Both the one who makes people holy and those who are made holy are of the same family. So Jesus is not ashamed to call them brothers and sisters. (Hebrews 2:11)

We have been completely beautified by the blood of our Bridegroom. A total head-to-toe, soul and heart makeover. Whether you feel it or not, he has not only taken away *all* your sin, but also *all* your shame. So we can worship ("embrace" him) as if we never ever sinned! Embracing our Bridegroom: isn't that a beautiful picture of what worship truly is?

If your relationship with God were set to music, what genre of music would be playing? Would it be some grindy punk rock or heavy metal? A depressing country western? Some boring elevator music? Or a passionate love duet? The *Song of Songs* is that joyous duet that the King and the church ought to be singing together. King Jesus came to forgive and to heal our shame-infested souls. He promised that we could find rest for our troubled hearts and enjoy "a hundred times as much in this present age" (Matthew 11:28–30; Mark 10:28–31). Are you one of those "100 times as much" Christians? How about your marriage? Is it a "100 times as much" marriage? I know heaven is going to be filled with an inexpressible joy that never fades. But Jesus says that we can taste some of that glorious joy even now. Jesus' first picture of the kingdom was at that wedding in Cana where the whole community celebrated with two unashamed lovers who brilliantly pictured the King and his bride.

CHAPTER 2

Mystery

Whether you are single or married, sexually satisfied or sexually frustrated, sexually hopeful or sexually defeated, would you allow this song above all other songs to point you toward the beauty of sexual love inside the bonds of marriage and more significantly toward the lover of your soul, Jesus Christ? If we look at the big-picture message of the book of Song of Solomon—at the joy of sexual oneness in marriage—we see the physical expression of a spiritual reality.

Throughout the Bible we find that marriage is a metaphor for God's relationship to his people. It is not that God looked at a human invention marriage and decided that it would provide a good illustration he could use to communicate the relationship he intends to have with his people. Instead, God created marriage between a man and a woman with this very purpose in mind.

Marriage is not primarily about finding the love of your life who will make you happy. And the Bible's instructions about marriage are not provided primarily to ensure your personal fulfillment. If you are married, the reason you are married is so that you can put the covenant-keeping love of Christ for his church on display for the world to see. This infuses our ordinary marriages with sacred meaning and purpose.[5]

In this same way, husbands ought to love their wives as their own bodies. He who loves his wife loves himself. After all, no one ever hated their own body, but they feed and care for their body, just as Christ does the church— for we are members of his body. "For this reason a man will leave his father and mother and be united to his wife, and the two will become one flesh."

This is a profound mystery—but I am talking about Christ and the church. However, each one of you also must love his wife as he loves himself, and the wife must respect her husband. (Ephesians 5:28–33)

It is compelling that Paul, an expert ministry builder, spent so much time writing and teaching about marriage. Why does this single evangelist/preacher/teacher dig deep into marriage yet never mention the numerical growth of the church? Paul cared about evangelism (1 Corinthians 9:19; 1 Timothy 2:3–4), but he knew that a growing, Spirit-filled church could only be established by growing, Spirit-filled members. Certainly, bold evangelism is one way to be filled with the Spirit (Acts 4:8–31). However, it is not the only way. Overemphasizing evangelism while underemphasizing marriage health will eventually lead to discouraged members and stagnant growth. We can and should be relentlessly focused on both. Paul knew how to build a church that would last, and it included refusing to neglect the complicated needs of the marrieds ministry. A tension-filled, stressed-out, disconnected marriage ministry has the potential to set that same atmosphere for the entire church.

We need to examine where our picture of marriage comes from. Who painted your picture of what it means to be a husband or a wife? Why do you believe what you believe about marriage? What about the roles and responsibilities within marriage—what do you think they are and why do you picture them that way? Are these pictures of marriage painted by your culture? Are they painted by your parents? Are they painted by your own feelings and thinking? Take stock, be honest. Understand that only the Creator of marriage should be allowed to craft in our hearts what it means to be a husband or wife.

Let's dive into some of the Bible's profound truths about marriage.

When a husband loves his wife, he is loving himself. This is true because of what happened on their wedding day. What

God does on our wedding day is first taught in Genesis 2 and expanded upon by Jesus in Matthew 19.

> Some Pharisees came to him to test him. They asked, "Is it lawful for a man to divorce his wife for any and every reason?"
>
> "Haven't you read," he replied, "that at the beginning the Creator 'made them male and female,' and said, 'For this reason a man will leave his father and mother and be united to his wife, and the two will become one flesh'? So they are no longer two, but one flesh. Therefore what God has joined together, let no one separate." (Matthew 19:3–6)

The Bible teaches that once we are married, we are "no longer two" because God has joined us together. We may still be two separate bodies walking around, but in the deepest sense, God has joined our souls into one. God himself is three equal, sovereign beings who are intimately one; and marriage was created by God to reflect the bliss-filled oneness of the Godhead. This is a deeply profound truth. One of the most prevalent pictures in the Bible is of Jesus as our bridegroom King. Becoming a Christian is accepting this bloodstained marriage proposal, a proposal that will someday lead to an eternal honeymoon (Revelation 19:6–9, 21:1–22:21). Marriage as God intended it is a prophetic picture of our intimacy with Jesus Christ.

The epitome of intimacy is found within the Divine Family. As surprising as it may sound, bedroom intimacy plays a role in revealing what God is like. 1 Corinthians 6:15–17 teaches that "one flesh" is primarily about sex. Therefore, sex as God created it to be is one of the most powerful ways that profound mysteries about God are unveiled. Obviously, there is no physical intimacy with God, and there will be no sex in heaven. There will be no human marriage in the age to come (Luke 20:35). Just as the animal sacrifices were done away with at Jesus' resurrection, so will the symbol of marriage become obsolete at his second coming. What is most exciting is that the symbol is always far outmatched by the reality that it points to. What we will have with King Jesus in our eternal marriage to him will far exceed any intimate pleasures we have enjoyed in this present age. Every obstacle that hinders our intimacy now will be completely removed. Our future relationship with each other will not include sex because we will have something far better. I can't even imagine that!

When Paul got a glimpse of the future glories awaiting us, he was forbidden to describe what he saw (2 Corinthians 12:1–10). He wasn't allowed to share about his "surpassingly great revelations" because human language falls pathetically short in describing what is in our future. Sexual joy is one of the greatest pleasures two human beings can experience. But that joy will be replaced by a much greater and much more fulfilling eternal intimacy with King Jesus.

This is why Satan despises and works to destroy marriages. He does not want us to understand profound mysteries about our future with Jesus, our bridegroom King. Have you ever felt that there is an insidious force fighting against you and your spouse? Your hunch is correct. Satan hates marriage and hates sex. You might be thinking that the devil loves sex. After all, the porn industry rakes in billions of dollars every year. But that isn't sex. It is a selfish, greedy distortion of one of God's most precious gifts. Because there are so many biblical prohibitions surrounding sex, many have jumped to the false conclusion that it can't be a holy aspect of God's plan for his people. Nothing could be further from the truth. There were many regulations that guided our old covenant brothers concerning temple worship, especially animal sacrifices. The myriad rules were there not because God was down on these things. These sacrifices were supremely holy because of what they symbolized. The same is true of sex. The many warnings in the Bible about sex are there precisely because this form of intimacy is so holy. Sex was created by God to teach us something about him. So Satan must find a way to ruin this highly instructive gift. He doesn't want you to see God as a sacred pleasure. In his attempt to destroy intimacy, he does everything he can to get you to have sex before you are married. After you are married, he does everything he can to get you not to enjoy it. That's because sex is so holy it can either delight or destroy us.

In teaching the church at Ephesus how to be filled with the Spirit, Paul says they should instruct one another with "psalms, hymns, and songs from the Spirit." One of the most important steps in becoming a Spirit-filled church is to be deeply educated by the poetry and songs of the Bible. Poetry is the language of passion and therefore can illuminate the soul in ways that ordinary language cannot. It is a compelling fact that about 30 percent of the Bible is poetry. Within the Bible's songs, there are many rich metaphors engineered to help us understand and know God more intimately.

I learned to appreciate poetry firsthand when I attended a poetry slam at my daughter's college. One of the performers recited a poem about a woman who had been terribly abused. It was gut-wrenching. She executed the poem with such raw emotion that it became clear it was written about herself. To this day, many years later, I still boil with emotion when I think about the poetic portrayal of her suffering. Poetry communicates the language of emotions in a visceral way that other forms of communication cannot.

Many of us were taught to disconnect visceral emotions from God. Some of us have even been conditioned to believe that any emotion that is too strong is evil. But this is simply untrue. God wants very much for us to develop passionate feelings for him (Psalms 18:1, 27:4, 42:1–2, 63:1–11, 84:1–2, 143:6). His desire for an intimate relationship with us is expressed in the language of the Bible's poetry.

The poetry of Scripture also reveals the deep things within the heart of God (1 Corinthians 2:9–12). God did not create us because he was lonely. King Jesus did not die for us because he can't live without us. It was out of pure love, not desperation or neediness, that God created us and is willing to re-create us through salvation. The passion of God led to the passion of the Christ. This depth of desire and love is revealed in the *Song of Songs*.

When we see that the lovesick king in the *Song of Songs* is a picture of King Jesus' longings for us, our relationship with God can become dominated by love, not legalism. I used to think that all God really cared about was that I got my Christian duties done. Now I see that what he wanted more than anything else was me. I eagerly do what pleases, not out of insecurity, but out of profound gratitude and with great joy. In that kind of relational atmosphere, the Holy Spirit can do his best work. Someday we will be in a constant state of spiritual inebriation. But that intimate intoxication can even overtake us now as we read, study, and sing the great songs of Scripture.

The section on marriage in Ephesians 5 ends with a practical challenge to marrieds in the church:

> Each one of you also must love his wife as he loves himself,
> and the wife must respect her husband. (Ephesians 5:33)

Each husband should love his wife and each wife should respect her husband. Why is that true? So married people can feel fulfilled and be happy? That may be so, but it isn't the reason Paul gives us in this passage. The reason every husband should selflessly love his wife and every wife should intensely admire her husband is so that together they can be a prophetic picture of the church's relationship with Christ. *This is the ultimate purpose of marriage.*

We should teach our young people what many of us were never taught before we were married. I was ill prepared for marriage, and because of that, Kelli and I struggled for years.

Husbands were created to be a safe place of never-diminishing love, and wives were created to be a source of consistent admiration for their husbands. How different would your marriage be if you saw it not as a way to get your personal needs met but as a covenant-partnership, meant to display the faithful love God shows to his people (the husband's role)? And how the people should gratefully respond (the wife's role)?

Of course, this is quite difficult in everyday life. Both souls in a marriage must endure the process of many painful experiences during their union. Each season of life brings bigger and different challenges. Living in a fallen world alongside other sinful people will require many "crucifixions" to learn to love like Jesus loves. But within a marriage, the Holy Spirit is ignited by selfless love and undeserved admiration. As each husband and each wife wholeheartedly submits to their God-ordained calling, the Holy Spirit can transform their marriages to become prophetic beacons of grace. Over time, these godly marriages can have an intoxicating effect within the whole church and attract others to the fellowship. If great mysteries about Jesus Christ can be revealed in the Old Testament sacrificial system through the sacrifice of common farm animals, think of the even deeper mysteries that can be discovered through the extraordinary marriages of ordinary people who are willing to "submit...out of reverence for Christ" (Ephesians 5:21) and "love...as Christ loved the church" (Ephesians 5:25).

CHAPTER 3

Image

God is not a single person, an individual in cool detachment from other persons. God is three persons in the deepest possible communion with each other. They have quite separate identities. The Father is the Father, not Son or Spirit. The Son's identity is his alone, he is never Father or Spirit. And the Spirit's self is unique, too. These persons are more distinct from each other than we can begin to understand or imagine. They don't merge or blend into a single personality. And yet, they are so intimate to each other, so present within each other, that they are only one God—not three. In their knowing and loving of each other, they hold nothing back for themselves. The Father abandons his entire self to his Son and Spirit, and Son and Spirit do the same. The love that circulates among them is so perfect that their communion with each other is perfect too. That is the kind of God that we believe in. We cannot understand such unity among such distinctive persons. But that is the mystery we believe.[6]

Image bearers—that is what human beings were created to be. This is a truth couched within the first chapter of the God story, and this story graciously includes all of us.

> Then God said, "Let us make mankind in our image, in our likeness, so that they may rule over the fish in the sea and the birds in the sky, over the livestock and all the wild animals, and over all the creatures that move along the ground."

> So God created mankind in his own image,
> in the image of God he created them;
> male and female he created them.

> God blessed them and said to them, "Be fruitful and in-
> crease in number; fill the earth and subdue it. Rule over the fish
> in the sea and the birds in the sky and over every living creature
> that moves on the ground." (Genesis 1:26–28)

"Let *us* make mankind in our image." The eternal Divine Family that created us is a wonder to behold. One God, three persons. Not three Gods—one God. It's a head-scratcher. What will really make you scratch your noggin is that these three all-powerful, equal, diverse beings have never experienced the slightest discord or distance within their relationship. There is no friction, no infighting, no jealousy, no competition, nor anything similar. What is more, they are in their sacred community of their own free will. None of them are robots.

> "The reason my Father loves me is that I lay down my life—
> only to take it up again. No one takes it from me, but I lay it down
> of my own accord. I have authority to lay it down and authority
> to take it up again. This command I received from my Father."
> (John 10:17–18)

God desired that Jesus, his beloved Son, would die for this world. Jesus, however, had complete freedom to choose whether to be crucified. One of the greatest reasons the Father is so well pleased with his Son is because he sacrificed his own freedom for the good of others. This passage reveals that God is a community of freewill beings. The perfect unity they have always shared is not programmed or coerced in any way.

None of the members of this bliss-filled family are weak, timid, or mousy. You might even say they tend to be of a "type A" temperament. Father, Son, and Spirit are opinionated yet always unified. Put three highly opinionated humans in the same room together, and it will only take a few minutes before they are arguing about religion or politics. There is a structure within the Godhead that includes authority and submission, but I will write about that controversial topic in the next chapter.

So how do these equal, strong-willed, completely free beings always remain one in everything that they dream and do? If we can specifically answer that question, then I think we can discover what it primarily means to be an image bearer.

The answer to the above question is simple but difficult. God is love (1 John 4). Love is the glue that cements the Divine Family together. But to be effective image bearers, we must properly define love. The word "love" is thrown around so indiscriminately that we must make sure we understand the kind of love God calls us to.

God is love, SO GOD IS ALWAYS SELFLESS. Search with all your might, and you will never find a moment in the gospels when the Son of God thought of himself first. You will find times when he was sorely tempted with selfishness, but he never submitted to his flesh (Matthew 4:1–11, 26:36–46). The battle that raged within him was so intense that he often prayed with "loud cries and tears" (Hebrews 5:7–9 ESV). Yet the Lord never caved in to those ferocious desires. Every day he fought to be selfless and won. Consider this: he had no advantage over us because of his identity as God. He set aside all the advantages of his equality with God (Philippians 2). He was fully God but also fully human. He fought against Satan and sin as a human being. Therefore, he is our pioneer in the faith and the example of victory over relentlessly self-focused sin.

At the last supper, King Jesus was bone weary and emotionally distraught. I have wondered how he got any sleep that week, knowing that he was going to be brutally crucified on the Passover (John 18:4). His best friends were completely out of touch with how lonely and discouraged he was. An argument even broke out among them regarding who was the greatest (Luke 22:24). Jesus portrayed pure selflessness amid rank selfishness. The Son was already suffering and quite possibly tempted to quit. Instead, this amazing man picked up a towel and served.

I think the most difficult part for Jesus was not the dirt and grime, but the intense loneliness. Suffering is always difficult. But suffering alone amid friends who seem out of touch is the worst. His loneliness would become even more acute just a few hours later when he prayed alone in the company of three sleeping disciples. Then, at his darkest hour, they fled the scene and left the one person who always loved them to walk the last steps to the cross alone. Please do not misunderstand my criticism of the twelve. I know I would have betrayed him too.

This perfect, ever-present selflessness is the atmosphere in which the Father, Son, and Holy Spirit exist eternally. One of the chief reasons they are always one is because they never think of themselves first. The overwhelming, unfulfilled needs that Jesus experienced the last week of his life did not stop him from loving the same people who neglected those very needs. He could have thrown the biggest pity party of all time. But because of his great love for the Father and his children, he loved them to the end (John 13:1).

> "Be dressed ready for service and keep your lamps burning, like servants waiting for their master to return from a wedding banquet, so that when he comes and knocks they can immediately open the door for him. It will be good for those servants whose master finds them watching when he comes. Truly I tell you, he will dress himself to serve, will have them recline at the table and will come and wait on them. It will be good for those servants whose master finds them ready, even if he comes in the middle of the night or toward daybreak." (Luke 12:35–38)

Have you ever read a passage in the Bible and felt like a big fist came up out of the page and punched you right in the face? I read through the above verses for years and never noticed something profound. But one day, that fist hit me. What is King Jesus going to be doing in the age to come? Sitting on his throne being worshiped around the clock? He deserves that, but that isn't the picture that this verse reveals. Luke writes that our selfless

Savior is going to be waiting on us as we recline. Whether that is what will literally happen or is a metaphor, I am not sure. The point is, in heaven the King will still be serving, a surprising truth that should not be so surprising if we understand that the core of the Father, Son, and Holy Spirit is true selflessness and love.

God is love, so God is *completely humble.* God has no ego. Even a microscopic speck of pride has a spoiling effect on love. God's love is untainted by any form of arrogance.

> "Come to me, all you who are weary and burdened, and I will give you rest. Take my yoke upon you and learn from me, for I am gentle and humble in heart, and you will find rest for your souls. For my yoke is easy and my burden is light." (Matthew 11:28–30)

> In your relationships with one another, have the same mindset as Christ Jesus:

> Who, being in very nature God,
>   did not consider equality with God something to be used
> to his own advantage;
>   rather, he made himself nothing
>   by taking the very nature of a servant,
>   being made in human likeness.
> And being found in appearance as a man,
>   he humbled himself
>   by becoming obedient to death—
>   even death on a cross! (Philippians 2:5–8)

Only Jesus could declare that he was "humble in heart" without it being at least subtly prideful. Even though God has a thick resume full of perfect and powerful accomplishments, there is not a hint of conceit within the Divine Community. Can you even imagine a fellowship of people where there is no pride at all?

Can you imagine being able to speak a universe into existence out of nothing and not being even slightly arrogant? Or being completely holy yet never self-righteous? Can you imagine your own image bearers that you created out of the dust irreverently thumbing their noses up at you, and you never responding out of pride, only concern?

To me, the most impressive thing about the Almighty is that he has no ego at all. The Divine Three created galaxies with ease. It only took a little bit of his breath to create everything and everyone. Yet all seven billion of us together with all our human wisdom, strength, and ingenuity combined couldn't even create a toothpick.

It is completely ludicrous for any man or woman to struggle with pride. The sins of arrogance are of the sneakiest variety. A person can be very humble in one area yet prideful in another. Married couples often struggle with this, being humble with others yet prideful with one another. Being defensive, overly opinionated, unapologetic, and insecure are manifestations of this intimacy-killing sin. An unwillingness to change and follow God's plan for what it means to be a wife or a husband is another way this sin rears its ugly head. Having a better idea than God about intimate issues is always pride.

> When he had finished washing their feet, he put on his clothes and returned to his place. "Do you understand what I have done for you?" he asked them. "You call me 'Teacher' and 'Lord,' and rightly so, for that is what I am. Now that I, your Lord and Teacher, have washed your feet, you also should wash one another's feet. I have set you an example that you should do as I have done for you. Very truly I tell you, no servant is greater than his master, nor is a messenger greater than the one who sent him. Now that you know these things, you will be blessed if you do them." (John 13:12–17)

Jesus knew exactly who he was when he humbly washed the

apostles' feet and submitted himself to the crucifixion. People he created pounded nails through his body. Men to whom he gave the breath of life spit in his face. What kind of all-powerful Creator would allow such a thing to happen? A completely humble one! So the second ingredient of love that holds the Godhead forever together as one is humility.

God is love, SO GOD IS ALWAYS PASSIONATE. True love, biblical love, is fiery. God is a jealous God, a consuming fire (Deuteronomy 4:24). It is true that love is more than a feeling. However, I do not teach anymore that love is not a feeling. Let it be known that the Divine Family is full of zealous feelings for each other and for every one of us.

"I am consumed with passion for Jerusalem!" (Zechariah 8:2 NLT)

God wasn't madly in love with the streets and buildings of Jerusalem, he was burning with passion for his people, his bride. Even more incredible, by the time God makes this proclamation of love, his bride has been adulterous for a long time. Can you imagine having possessive emotions like that for your wife even after discovering she has been unfaithful many times? Such is the unexplainable love of God.

Study the book of Hosea and you will be convinced to the core of your being that the Bridegroom has passionate feelings for you. You will see him as your spiritual Husband that gets red-faced in rage at anything that threatens your marriage. One of the Hebrew words that is translated "jealousy" means to be red-faced in anger. In the human arena, jealousy is often a destructive sin. However, with God it is a manifestation of the depth of his love for us. If someone openly flirted with a man's wife while he was having dinner with her, and he showed no jealousy, that would be a sign of shallowness on his part. It would reveal that his wife and their relationship wasn't that important to him. The perfect consistency of God's love never diminishes, so his feelings for us never diminish. God's holy love is a raging, consuming fire. This is so true of him that his name is Jealous! (Exodus 34:14).

This aching desire that we be wholly his led King Jesus to his crucifixion. And God's willingness to do whatever it took to remove any obstacle should inspire us to do the same. King Jesus is, by far, the most attractive and eligible bachelor available to all of us. Instead, many of us love money, possessions, other people, and ourselves more than him. We are deceived, like Eve, that God is not all that awesome and that there may be "somebody" or "something" better out there. As the bride of Christ, we should understand that even a hint of flirtation with another suitor is unacceptable. It is easy to imagine that Adam and Eve were taking flirtatious glances at the tree before they caved in to Satan's seductive temptations. They were most likely lusting after what God had said was forbidden.

In a sense, Satan destroyed them through pornography. Pornography creates passion for somebody or something else and therefore ruins your passion for your spouse and your God. It often begins subtly, with lingering looks at racy commercials or tantalizing social media content. The devil is a patient hunter, and we must always be alert and extremely careful.

Now let's examine what may be the greatest definition ever penned about what love is.

> Set me as a seal upon your heart,
>   as a seal upon your arm,
> for love is strong as death,
>   jealousy is fierce as the grave.
> Its flashes are flashes of fire,
>   the very flame of the LORD.
> Many waters cannot quench love,
>   neither can floods drown it.
> If a man offered for love
>   all the wealth of his house,

he would be utterly despised. (Song of Songs 8:6–7 ESV)

The above verse describes the kind of covenant love that creates security in a bride. At this point in the poetic narrative, Solomon's wife needs some reassurance that he will continue to love her in this fashion. Men are called by God to be the keepers and guardians of the marriage covenant. And the covenant is all about how you love. As we study this passage, it will become obvious that this scripture also describes God's love for his bride, a love that men are called to imitate, a love that creates radiant brides.

For "love is strong as death." What a strange metaphor. Death never quits, and neither does genuine love. Death never looks at some kale-eating workout fanatic and throws up his hands saying, "This guy is just too determined to live. I quit!" No matter how healthy a person is, death is inevitable. Last time I checked, the mortality rate is 100 percent.

I have seen couples quit on each other for relatively minor issues. I have also seen couples refuse to quit even after adultery could have broken them apart. Unbelievably, some of the strongest marriages I know have suffered and overcome infidelity. God gave Hosea the heart-wrenching challenge to not quit on his prostitute wife. Only that depth of hurt and love could reveal the true scale of God's own love for his people (Hosea 2–3).

If you are in a difficult marriage, it may be because God desires that you display his relentless covenant love. We live in a world full of quitters; don't be one! My wife and I have counseled several situations that involved adultery. Only one time did I believe divorce was the best option. God certainly allows divorce when the covenant vows have been broken through infidelity. But our God is one of forgiveness and restoration, and he always hates divorce, no matter the reason (Malachi 2:16 NASB).

Today, too many Christians choose divorce for shallow or selfish reasons. In the Old Testament, God allowed some divorce for grounds other than adultery. But in Matthew 19 Jesus explains that that concession is now over. Now that he has arrived, has given his life on the cross, and has sent the Holy Spirit to dwell within us, we have everything we need for our hearts to be transformed (2 Peter 1:3–11).

The Holy Spirit longs to teach us how to love like death! People who assume love should be easy don't even know what love is. The only way to learn to love like death is to die to yourself.

"Jealousy is fierce as the grave." Another strange and powerful metaphor. Here is what I believe it means: the grave wants you exclusively for itself. The grave will not share you with life in any way. You cannot hold hands with life and with the grave at the same time. We only bury people who have no life within them. Married love is to be exclusive love. Even if you have children, the person you are called to love the most in this life is your spouse.

In the last fifty years the United States has become a kid-centric society. In many homes the children have become the center around which all else revolves. This is an unhealthy paradigm that has the potential to create a society full of entitled children. I'm not blaming the kids; it is the parents who are at fault. This thinking has a huge impact on the quality of marriage after kids arrive. Stressed-out moms and dads drive little Johnny everywhere because he has to be in every club, every sport, and every activity possible, otherwise he won't grow up to be a well-rounded person. The best thing parents can do for their children is to love God and each other exclusively. Your child will not die if you don't go to every sporting event. Furthermore, if you make life so awesome for your kids, will they want to seek God ? The mindset that "my kids have to have it better than I did" is only sometimes a good way to think. Your kids will grow up and leave you for somebody else, and then it will be just you and that person you're married to. There's a growing trend of people getting divorced after becoming empty nesters because of the very thing that we just talked about. Putting your marriage on the back burner while raising kids is a horrible decision. A husband and wife who are crazy about each other can love their children even more. And children of such parents feel much more secure in a home with an atmosphere like that.

Here is one more metaphor about love from the *Song of Songs*: "Love is...the very flame of the Lord." God is love. Completely and thoroughly passionate love. He is saturated, drenched, engulfed, and raging with perfect, selfless, humble love. His love for you never smolders or flickers (Malachi 3:6; Hebrews 13:8). He is obsessed with us. This depth of love is the only explanation for the crucifixion.

God is always on fire for you. He may not always be fired up about what you do, but he is always deeply in love with you. He loves you when you are doing awesome spiritually, and he loves you when you are stumbling. He loves you before, during, and after you sin. This is why it says in Hebrews chapter four that we can "approach God's throne of grace with confidence." In no way am I trying to say that we should be sloppy in our obedience or presume upon his amazing grace. But knowing, really knowing, that the sovereign Creator of the universe always loves you like this will create a raging fire within your soul for him. He loves it when you are on fire for him.

The tachometer on my 1994 Kawasaki Concourse redlines at about 10,500 rpms. In sixth gear at just 4000 rpms I am cruising at around 70 miles an hour. I have never even been close to the redline. I've only occasionally visited 7000 rpms when I am in a hurry to pass a big truck. But I have only stayed there momentarily. Younger motorcyclists would say I drive  my bike like an old man. This is true, because I am an old man and I don't want to get hurt.

You see, when you bury the needle into the redline you are much more likely to crash and burn. But none of us should love in the way I drive my Kawasaki. When we first became Christians, most of us buried the needle into the redline for God and others. This also happened when you were first married. But then you got hurt, and because you suffered some spiritual road rash, you backed off and are now cruising safely far away from the redline. This happens to everyone except our God.

I believe in necessary boundaries, but sometimes we can overdo boundaries and use them as an excuse to not risk ourselves by loving selflessly. King Jesus is incapable of backing off in his love for us. And because of that, he crashed and burned on a cross. True love suffers much, but true love will always have the most incredible outcome. Whether in this life or in the next, this kind of passionate love will be rewarded richly by God. Oftentimes it is apathy that keeps us from loving zealously. *But passionate feelings can be resurrected through passionate actions.* That is why the Bible says that when we are trying to overcome apathy we should go and do the things we did at first (Revelation 2:1–7).

"Many waters cannot quench...neither can floods drown" or dilute covenant love. God has endured floods of trouble from his bride. If you look at the history of Israel, or even our personal history, we know in our souls that we do not deserve to be loved in the way God loves us. If you pitted the greatest of all California fires against Niagara Falls in a contest, which of them would win? My family lived through a couple of those fires when we lived in California, and I also have visited Niagara Falls. No question about it, Niagara would come out victorious. Almost 3200 tons of water flows over the falls every second. Eventually water always wins, and that much wet stuff would win in a hurry. But not with God. His fiery love can never be drowned out. Every single day, he deals with a deluge of sin yet refuses to quit on us. Praise God that he is not a quitter. The key to developing this kind of love is found in the final thought from this passage: you cannot buy or earn this kind of love. The lover has to freely bless you with their selfless passion. Grace is the gift of loving those who do not deserve it. If we are only capable of loving when we believe our spouse deserves it, we are not loving with the grace of God. Our love is more selfish than passionate.

In these two verses that we have studied, the wife is basically saying, "Please, please, love me graciously. Please don't ask me to earn it. It will help me feel safe and secure if you learn to consistently love me this way." Just a few verses later, she promises to give her husband the same kind of love.

> I was a wall,
>> and my breasts were like towers;
> then I was in his eyes
>> as one who finds peace.
> Solomon had a vineyard at Baal-hamon;
>> he let out the vineyard to keepers;
>> each one was to bring for its fruit a thousand pieces of
> silver.
> My vineyard, my very own, is before me;
>> you, O Solomon, may have the thousand,
>> and the keepers of the fruit two hundred.
>> (Song of Songs 8:10–12)

Solomon rented his vineyard in Baal-hamon to some farmers. Each farmer was charged 1000 shekels of silver to live on and work his property. The Shulammite also had a vineyard, which was not only her body, but her entire self (Song of Songs 1:6, 4:12–16). In this little piece of poetry, Solomon's wife assures him that he does not have to "pay" for her love. Her affection does not need to be earned. Her "vineyard" is free; he can keep his 1000 shekels. And because she has learned to live that way, her husband has found great contentment within their relationship.

How does this amazing, divine community we know as God always remain unified in the deepest possible ways, in everything they dream and do? How do they stay so intimately connected to one another? They are bound together by this kind of love, which each of them lives for and gives away. Each member of this divine community is voluntarily and perfectly selfless, humble, and passionate. A family of image bearers on earth imitating this same love is what Jesus was praying for right before he was crucified.

> "My prayer is not for them alone. I pray also for those who will believe in me through their message, that all of them may be one, Father, just as you are in me and I am in you. May they also be in us so that the world may believe that you have sent me. I have given them the glory that you gave me, that they may be one as we are one— I in them and you in me—so that they may be brought to complete unity. Then the world will know that you sent me and have loved them even as you have loved me." (John 17:20–23)

If you want to know what King Jesus desires most, then study the greatest of all prayers, which is recorded in John 17. What you will discover is that Jesus wants us to be a community just like them. As vital as forgiveness is, Jesus didn't die just to erase our sins. He died to make the entire world unified again, as it was at the beginning. Practically, the only way this can happen is if we intentionally and with great perseverance imitate the love that we just studied. Even now, a sincere church is marching toward the great unity to come, by imitating the sacrificial love of God. Can you imagine an entire church that is dominated by this kind of love? Or can you imagine a small group where everybody is devoted to being selfless, humble, and always passionate for each other? And where would all this begin within a church community? Wouldn't it be in the most fundamental building block of any society? Yes, the individual families and homes within the church. And at the helm of every family is a husband and a wife. A mom and a dad. Can you imagine how powerful one married couple could be if they were consistently saturated with the selfless, humble, and never-apathetic love that is a constant state within the Godhead? The ripples from their love would affect generations. This special love would increase the flow of relational wine even before the glorious return of our Bridegroom (John 17:13). And more and more people would be attracted to this loving and joyous fellowship (Isaiah 55:5, 61:9; Jeremiah 33:9). An uncommon joy would be created by this image-bearing love. Now you and I know at least a little of what it means to image the Divine Family. This is why we were created.

CHAPTER 4

Roles

Maleness and femaleness mean something very important in the Bible, something non-negotiable. There's no notion of a unisex, roleless marriage.[7]

So God created mankind in his own image,
in the image of God he created them;
male and female he created them. (Genesis 1:27)

Gender roles are a hot topic these days. In this chapter I certainly will not answer many of the questions that surround this important subject. However, we will explore some of the fundamental passages in the Bible that speak of gender-specific roles. In this book we will look at the roles of husbands and wives but will not treat the specifics of the women's role within the church family, which I know is another hot topic.

Reflecting God as human beings is not only about imaging the amazing love within God. We are also called to imitate the roles that are within the Divine Family. Let's take a peek at one of the most debated and hated passages in the Bible.

But I want you to realize that the head of every man is Christ, and the head of the woman is man, and the head of Christ is God. (1 Corinthians 11:3)

When you attempt to decipher what a passage like this means, it's important that you interpret it in light of the entire Bible. Furthermore, although culture has its place, we must be extremely careful in how we use it. Truly foundational things about life that are defined in Scripture should never be updated by cultural views. Sometimes we can flex with our culture and sometimes not. Bad theology promoted by shallow people who think they understand scriptures like this have done great damage. A woeful lack of reverence is the greatest reason why scriptures like this are so often misinterpreted (Isaiah 66:1–4). Previous hurts through the exercise of bad leadership, especially within marriage, can also make some resistant to seeing what these scriptures mean. In dealing with passages like this, we have to work hard to excavate only what the Bible is teaching.

Much of the controversy around this passage stems from the argument over what the word "head" means. Does it mean source, or authority? It is my understanding from what I have read that the Greek word could mean either. There are many very accomplished theologians on either side of the aisle concerning the meaning of this word. I hardly know any Greek, so I'm not going to join that debate.

This passage spins off the idea that we are image bearers even when it concerns our roles.

It seems to me that within the marriage relationship, the husband is in a similar role as the Father, and the wife is in a similar role as the Son. So let's do a little study on how the Father and Son relate to each other, and I think we can figure out what this passage truly means. We will look at several passages from the fourth gospel.

> Jesus gave them this answer: "Very truly I tell you, the Son can do nothing by himself; he can do only what he sees his Father doing, because whatever the Father does the Son also does. (John 5:19)

> By myself I can do nothing; I judge only as I hear, and my judgment is just, for I seek not to please myself but him who sent me. (5:30)

> I have come down from heaven not to do my will but to do

the will of him who sent me. (6:38)

Jesus answered, "My teaching is not my own. It comes from the one who sent me. Anyone who chooses to do the will of God will find out whether my teaching comes from God or whether I speak on my own. (7:16–17)

Jesus said, "When you have lifted up the Son of Man, then you will know that I am he and that I do nothing on my own but speak just what the Father has taught me. The one who sent me is with me; he has not left me alone, for I always do what pleases him." (8:28–29)

I did not speak on my own, but the Father who sent me commanded me to say all that I have spoken. I know that his command leads to eternal life. So whatever I say is just what the Father has told me to say." (12:49–50)

Don't you believe that I am in the Father, and that the Father is in me? The words I say to you I do not speak on my own authority. Rather, it is the Father, living in me, who is doing his work. Believe me when I say that I am in the Father and the Father is in me; or at least believe on the evidence of the works themselves. (14:10–11)

He comes so that the world may learn that I love the Father and do exactly what my Father has commanded me. (14:31)

From what we just studied, the Father is the authority figure between the Son and himself. *However, and this is very important,* because they are so completely selfless and void of any kind of pride, the thought of who is in charge never even crosses their minds. Jesus eagerly lives to bring glory to his Father. With those scriptures in mind, now let's go to the very beginning.

Some believe that there was no sense of authority and submission within the Divine Family before Jesus became a human, with no sense of any kind of hierarchy. At this point in my walk with God, I am not of that persuasion. This is primarily because of the teaching in 1 Corinthians 15. I am open to being in a different place in the future on this, but this is where I fall now.

> Then the end will come, when he hands over the kingdom to God the Father after he has destroyed all dominion, authority and power. For he must reign until he has put all his enemies under his feet. The last enemy to be destroyed is death. For he "has put everything under his feet." Now when it says that "everything" has been put under him, it is clear that this does not include God himself, who put everything under Christ. When he has done this, then the Son himself will be made subject to him who put everything under him, so that God may be all in all. (1 Corinthians 15:24–28)

Unless there is something I do not understand about the above passage, it appears that the Father is going to be the ultimate authority in the coming world. I believe there have always been different roles, including authority, within the Godhead. Their oneness of heart is voluntary and not robotic. As I said earlier in the previous chapter, because every member of the Divine Family is completely selfless, totally humble and never apathetic, "who's in charge" never enters their minds. We have never experienced what an arrangement like that feels like. Since Genesis 3, there has always been some selfishness, pride, and guardedness within every relationship or community we involve ourselves in. And most times, far more than we even realize.

It seems to me that when we orchestrate a structure to keep a church in line, we are focusing on the wrong things. Making sure the lines of authority are clearly established doesn't bring lasting health to a community. Such thinking is infantile. A husband who "clubs" his wife with Ephesians 5 is revealing a gross misunderstanding of what God is like. Jesus entered our humanity not to intimidate us with his authority, but rather to win our hearts through crucified living and dying. By the way, gentlemen, Ephesians 5:22–24 was written for our wives. Sometimes men act like it was primarily written for them, but this is an error. Husbands mustn't lead through hierarchy, but rather through agape.

> Then the LORD God formed a man from the dust of the ground and breathed into his nostrils the breath of life, and the man became a living being.
> Now the LORD God had planted a garden in the east, in Eden; and there he put the man he had formed. (Genesis 2:7–8)

Genesis chapter 1 is all about the immensity of God. Chapter 2 is all about God's intimacy. After forming all the animal and plant life, God sculpts a bit of clay into the form of a man. Then, as it literally says in Hebrew, God kisses him to life. In the New Testament there are three Greek words that are translated "worship." One means to honor or give reverence. This word is in the New Testament one time. Another word means to serve and is in the New Testament four times.

The last word means to kiss. This word is in the New Testament fifty-eight times. God deserves our reverence and service, but what he desires most is being "kissably close" to us (Psalms 42:1–2, 63:1).

I witnessed my wife giving birth to our three children, and the same thing happened each time. As soon as the doctor gave our newborn to Kelli she held our new little creation as closely as she could. We were created for intimacy. Life unravels when we are not deeply connected to God. And when we do not have a healthy relationship with God, it's nearly impossible to have healthy relationships with others. That is what Genesis 3 is all about.

God placed his newly formed man in a flourishing garden of holy pleasure. Remember, in the Hebrew language, "Eden" means pleasure. Mistakenly, we usually do not associate pleasure with holiness, or God. Yet Eden was a place of inexpressible joy. For some time, Adam existed in the garden in a face-to-face joyous relationship with the Father, Son, and Holy Spirit.

> The LORD God took the man and put him in the Garden of Eden to work it and take care of it. And the LORD God commanded the man, "You are free to eat from any tree in the garden; but you must not eat from the tree of the knowledge of good and evil, for when you eat from it you will certainly die." (Genesis 2:15–17)

God placed some huge responsibilities upon the first man. He was called to guard the garden of sacred pleasure. He was commissioned to make sure that no nasty critters would bring ruin on this most special place. The snake should have never been anywhere near his wife. Adam should have stomped on his head as soon as he slithered into the garden. Soon, the "last Adam" will do what the first Adam failed to do (Genesis 3:15; Romans 16:20). Adam wasn't charged to take care of plants. He was to passionately protect his wife. Instead he was passive. This was a failure of love, because there is nothing passive about true love.

He was to make sure that the same love that saturated the Godhead would continue to flourish in this bliss-filled garden. When God was convinced that Adam knew the kind of love that held the Divine Family together, Adam was granted a community of his own. Adam had everything he needed to fulfill his purpose as the world's first king (Psalms 8). God had prepared him well. What made the garden beautiful was the love that existed there, not the vegetation. The indescribable joy of our future Eden is not that the mountains will be taller or the sunsets brighter or the fruit tastier, but rather that perfect love will be restored. The bride of Christ can rest securely because she knows her King will never drop his guard.

Because God is love, all the relationships he has are based on free will. Love only truly exists if there is a choice given. Thirty-five years ago when I asked my wife to marry me, I gave her a choice. I must have caught her at a weak moment, because she said, "Yes!" Intimacy cannot be forced or coerced, it must be freely given. This is also true concerning our gender-specific roles. The function of the tree of knowledge was to give the first humans a choice. God gives you the freedom to choose—he will not force you to love him or into the role that you were designed for. Life goes so much better when we voluntarily love him and eagerly embrace his gender-specific assignments (Isaiah 48:17–18). As long as Adam continued to make God-defined choices, he would continue to enjoy unrestricted fellowship with God. God makes it unmistakably clear that if Adam breaks the covenant he has initiated with him, it will result in certain death. In no way did Adam feel that God was a harsh taskmaster or control freak, since he was only charged to stay away from one tree.

All the other trees, most likely thousands of them, were available for his nourishment. Any thought that God is stingy is a false charge. God longs to be gracious to us (Isaiah 30:18). Adam was truly in the land of plenty with only one prohibition. Adam and Eve are the only human beings who have seen God face to face. They knew God in ways that we could only imagine...or better said, can't imagine. They must have seen how the Eternal Family functioned together seamlessly within their different roles. When you know God as deeply as they must have, you don't need a plethora of rules to regulate your relationship.

It was only after the intimacy was broken to pieces (Genesis 3) that God had to add hundreds of protective commands. However, God longs for the healing of our intimacy so that the depth of our relationship rules the day, not the rules (Jeremiah 31).

In my marriage to my wife, there are rules in the background that I never have to think about. I do not have to remind myself not to flirt with other women, because our feelings for each other are so deep. Temptations like that don't even enter my mind, and if they did, I wouldn't even consider them. God wants that kind of relationship with us (Colossians 2:16–23).

> The LORD God said, "It is not good for the man to be alone. I will make a companion for him who corresponds to him." (Genesis 2:18 NET)

When the time was right, God put the "first Adam" into a deep sleep. *Then he pierced his side to create his bride.* In the future he would do the same thing to the "last Adam" (John 19:34; 1 Corinthians 15:45).

Here's a thought-provoking question: did God create Eve because Adam was lonely or because he was alone? It is my strong opinion that he created the woman because Adam was alone. He was living in the immediate presence of God, so how could he have been lonely? Is that why there is no human marriage in the age to come? Will we be so full of God that it will completely supersede marriage as we know it in this present age? I can't definitively answer those questions. However, I know that in the future we will not struggle with any disappointment. Among other things, loneliness will disappear forever through our marriage to Jesus. So, it appears that the reason God created Eve was because Adam was alone. There was no way Adam by himself could image the Divine Family, so God yanked something out of him to create the first human community. To ensure that this first human family would truly reflect God, the Author of life created someone radically different from Adam. And their differences were much more than skin deep. God perfectly designed her to fulfill a different role than the man.

If Adam fulfilled his task in protecting the garden of selfless, humble, and passionate love, then this tiny community could picture God. Also, the perfect, inexpressible pleasure would remain and eventually fill the whole earth through their offspring.

It takes both genders to truly reflect the relationship between Father and Son. God did not make another man but someone quite different from man. The only way to truly image God is to be in a diverse community. This is true whether we are talking about marriage or the family of God, the church. People of the same gender in marriage cannot image God. That is one of the reasons why homosexual relationships are not considered a biblical marriage. This is also true on the larger scale with the church family. Is an all-white church in a diverse city an image-bearing community? I would say only if they are aggressively repenting of their lack of diversity. A diversity of persons flourishing in a selfless community is the heart and soul of what it means to image God. And this all starts in marriage, the most fundamental unit of society. It seems to me that if we can make this most intimate—and therefore difficult—relationship work, then we have a chance at reflecting God on every level.

In Genesis 2:18 the Hebrew says something like, "I will make someone very different from him, who will strengthen him." That's why she was a suitable helper. Eve was created to strengthen her man so he in turn could continue to protect the garden. The same Hebrew word translated "helper" is used of God often in the Old Testament (Deuteronomy 33:29; Ps 33:20).

> Once you spoke in a vision,
>> to your faithful people you said:
> "I have bestowed strength on a warrior;
>> I have raised up a young man from among the people.
> I have found David my servant;
>> with my sacred oil I have anointed him.
> My hand will sustain him;
>> surely my arm will strengthen him.
> The enemy will not get the better of him;
>> the wicked will not oppress him.
> I will crush his foes before him
>> and strike down his adversaries.

> My faithful love will be with him,
>> and through my name his horn will be exalted.
> I will set his hand over the sea,
>> his right hand over the rivers. (Psalm 89:19–25)

There is nothing demeaning about the woman's role in energizing her husband. The picture from Genesis 2 is not of a mop-carrying mom with her hair in a bun, three kids wrapped around her ankles, and beads of sweat on her forehead. And where is her husband? Lounging in a recliner asking for another beer. Shallow "theologians" came up with that interpretation. As God came alongside David and strengthened him to do battle, so a wife supplies energy for her covenant warrior. Ideally a husband has two main ways to be fortified for life: his two covenant partners, God and his bride. What a privilege to walk hand in hand with God to strengthen your man. So, my dear sisters, your chief role is not home floor care, but husband soul care. Women were crafted by God to nourish and nurture the souls of others. My wife always knows if there's something "off" about one of our kids or grandchildren. But men are experts at hiding their inner pain, because most of us were taught that to show any kind of weakness would make us a sissy. Even as little boys, many of us were scolded if we started to cry. "Stop being a baby!... Men don't cry.... Cut it out!... Quit being wimpy." In 2016 there were 45,000 suicides in the United States and nearly 80 percent were men. Since so many men are taught to stuff their feelings, could that be one of the chief reasons that so many take their lives? My point here is not to subtly blame women, but rather to point out that if your man seems OK, it doesn't mean he *is* OK. Without disrespect, criticism, frustration, or mothering, help him learn how to bring his troubled emotions to the surface when he is out of sorts. Many times when a man is angry it's because he is either hurt or discouraged. Often a quiet man is a hurting man. It's not always because "he's a man of few words, like his dad."

Of course, Adam needed to fulfill his role whether or not Eve accomplished hers. And this is true for all married men. It would just be far more difficult. More on that later.

> A man ought not to cover his head, since he is the image and glory of God; but woman is the glory of man. For man did not come from woman, but woman from man; neither was man created for woman, but woman for man. It is for this reason that a woman ought to have authority over her own head, because of the angels. Nevertheless, in the Lord woman is not independent of man, nor is man independent of woman. For as woman came from man, so also man is born of woman. But everything comes from God. (1 Corinthians 11:7–12)

"Hey, honey, how do you feel about being made for me, to bring me glory?" I recently asked my wife of thirty-five years that question. I braced myself for the answer, and she said, "Great!" Thank you, my dear Jesus, for the amazing wife you gave me. I do not deserve her. Of course, the passage above can be raped of its original meaning by either gender. Many people do not feel great about what this passage teaches, primarily because they don't really understand what it says and the beautiful fruit that can be produced if it is fully lived out. Man exists to bring glory only to God. So Eve living to bring glory to her husband is also about bringing glory only to God. There is nothing selfish or ego-tistical about the man's role. If there is, he is all about bringing glory to himself and not to his Head.

Jesus said clearly and often that he was not here to bring glory to himself. A man intensely focused on bringing glory to God with a wife living to strengthen him in that endeavor is what an image-bearing marriage is all about. That is what this passage is teaching. Domineering men who walk all over their wives are a horrible picture of God and a terrible advertisement for Christianity. Godly men see their wives as heroic and treat them with the greatest respect. I can't wait until we unpack Proverbs 31. We will get to those specifics later in the book.

Have you ever used a crescent wrench to pound in a nail? Because I seem to never be able to put my tools back where they belong, I have done that several times. I couldn't locate my hammer, so the wrench fulfilled a purpose it was not made for. Usually I bent a couple of nails and marred the wood in the process. Much of the stress in our modern society is because married people do not understand or do not want to live as they were created to be. I think this is true even in the church of Jesus Christ. Does the fragrance of your married ministry smell of peace and joy or frustration and stress? Are we letting culture define what a husband or wife is supposed to be? The secular world is never going to get these things right. We still have much to study about how to be effective image bearers. But let it be known that if we do not fulfill these fundamental roles, we will ruin the intoxicating effects of the Spirit. Jesus said, "I have come that they may have life, and have it to the full" (John 10:10). The gender-specific role differences are huge in reflecting God. We cannot mess with something that God has made so important and not expect to reap the misery-bringing results. Why is it that the average marriage only lasts six years? Why does the honeymoon always have to be over? Why are there so few older Christians who have passion-filled marriages? And why are there so many stressed-out families even within the church? Could it be that we need to go into the basement and check the foundation to make sure that we're building the church and our marriages as God desires? Just because much evil exists on the internet does not mean the internet is evil. Biblical roles are not bad just because they have been abused by foolish people. They are not the ancient way in need of being updated. Relationships always end up being discouraging or even destroyed by our insistence on doing things our own way. If a married couple will eagerly embrace the same love and the same roles that exist within the

Godhead, they will be richly blessed and prophetic. God has designed these fundamental things to bring us great joy. Defining gender roles as God does is of the utmost importance.

CHAPTER 5

Husbands

Jesus' love was a sacrificial love. It was an extravagant love. It was given to meet our needs, not to give him a warm and fuzzy feeling. He gave love to those who didn't want it, and he gave his love even though we didn't deserve it. That's the kind of love that is necessary if we are to learn to act right when our spouse acts wrong.[8]

Husbands, love your wives, just as Christ loved the church. (Ephesians 5:25)

Husbands were created by God to love, to be a forever safe place for their brides and children. Our wives should know they are unconditionally loved (Ephesians 5:25). This is how the ultimate bridegroom, King Jesus, has *always* loved us. Even though Jesus is holy and never sentimental, the "great sinners" of society felt safe with him (Mark 12:37; Matthew 11:19; Luke 7:36–50, 15:1–2). Adam was created to be a place of safety for his bride. Learning to lead is primarily about learning to love just like Jesus. Possessing excellent leadership skills while being anemic in love is fairly worthless (1 Corinthians 13:1–13), especially when it comes to marriage. It is often said that women are better at loving than men. I think this is true, but mostly because Satan has done his work so well. He has distracted men from their most important role in life. Christian men need to understand that their greatest calling in life is to become selfless, humble, and passionate imitators of King Jesus. To discover what it means to be a godly husband, we will look at the two great husbands of Scripture, King Jesus and King Solomon. Let us look at the ultimate Bridegroom first.

Gentlemen, get yourself ready, this will be extremely challenging. How has Jesus loved his bride?

JESUS

First, if the bride of Christ is thinking straight, she will be overwhelmed by the love of her bridegroom King.

So as a husband, I ask myself, is Kelli overwhelmed by my love for her? Sadly, for years my wife was underwhelmed by my love. And I think this is experienced far too often in marriages. Men love their jobs, their money, their hobbies, fishing, hunting, football, and even ministry more than their wives. At the last supper, when Jesus made the outlandish statement that he loved his disciples just like the Father loved him, no one rolled their eyes or shook their head. He really did, and they knew it was true. How can I as a flawed sinner love my wife in a way that overwhelms her? I must be relentless in my imitation of King Jesus. That is the only way. You or I will never follow Jesus perfectly, but we can do it consistently. Men, we do not have to help plant a church in a developing country to be a radical disciple. A man loving his wife consistently like Jesus is a radical Christian. And one of the signs that you are loving your wife like Jesus is that she is overwhelmed. I mean that in a good way. In the greatest book ever written about marriage, *Song of Songs,* the bride is consistently intoxicated (Song of Songs 1:2, 2:3–4, 5:8, 7:9–10) by the love of her husband. Men, it is our job to make sure our marriages don't become mediocre. King Jesus hates mediocrity, and so should we (Revelation 3:15–16). Leadership is primarily about example setting, not commanding. As we look at the greatest example of what it means to be a husband, King Jesus our Bridegroom, although I could share many things about his love, I will limit myself to two: his gracious love and his vow keeping.

GRACIOUS LOVE

Jesus' only response to anything was love. That certainly

doesn't mean everybody is saved, but it does mean anybody can be. Our Lord never stopped loving people regardless of how he was treated. For me, King Jesus has always been a rock, even when I have been a wreck. He is a huge boulder of grace, patience, and encouragement, especially when I don't deserve that kind of love. Even though he has never sinned in our relationship, he never holds grudges against me when I sin. It is amazing what the King of holiness is willing to forgive.

God forgave King Manasseh even after decades of flagrant defiance (2 Chronicles 33). Israel's spiritual husband was willing to forgive her for years of spiritual prostitution if she would just repent of her ways and become a genuine wife (Hosea). King Jesus forgave Saul of Tarsus even though he had murdered many Christians (Acts 26:9–11; 1 Timothy 1:12–17). A marriage can only reveal profound mysteries about God if both husband and wife become experts in forgiveness. And since we husbands are the leaders, we are called to lead the way in graciousness.

Jesus said to his disciples: "Things that cause people to stumble are bound to come, but woe to anyone through whom they come. It would be better for them to be thrown into the sea with a millstone tied around their neck than to cause one of these little ones to stumble. So watch yourselves.

"If your brother or sister sins against you, rebuke them; and if they repent, forgive them. Even if they sin against you seven times in a day and seven times come back to you saying 'I repent,' you must forgive them."

The apostles said to the Lord, "Increase our faith!"

He replied, "If you have faith as small as a mustard seed, you can say to this mulberry tree, 'Be uprooted and planted in the sea,' and it will obey you.

"Suppose one of you has a servant plowing or looking after the sheep. Will he say to the servant when he comes in from the field, 'Come along now and sit down to eat'? Won't he rather say, 'Prepare my supper, get yourself ready and wait on me while

I eat and drink; after that you may eat and drink'? Will he thank
the servant because he did what he was told to do? So you also,
when you have done everything you were told to do, should say,
'We are unworthy servants; we have only done our duty.'" (Luke
17:1–10)

In the above passage Jesus talks about radical forgiveness.
Even though this passage is not specifically about marriage, we
will use it in that way. What if your spouse sinned against you
seven times in one day? How would you respond to that kind
of treatment? If they are willing to respond to an honest and
loving correction (rebuke), we are called to completely forgive.
The offer of forgiveness should always be there even if they don't
repent.

Let me tell you a true story about a young couple I recently studied the Bible with. When Michael and Jenny (not their
real names) came to our church, they were already experienc-
ing a lot of trouble in their new marriage. Jenny very quickly
embraced the truth and became a Christian. However, Michael
was very displeased and became increasingly violent. Initially
he was quite interested, but after his wife joined our church he
became resentful. He stopped responding to my calls and re-
fused to study the Bible further. Because Jenny felt that she was
in danger, I counseled her to move out. I instructed her from the
Scriptures to never retaliate and to always remain calm and loving. She communicated with him that she loved him and would
continue to commit her life to him if he would stop behaving
in destructive ways. She let him know in many ways that she
forgave him. Her immense grace won him over, and now he is a
disciple of Christ and a loving husband.

After Jesus teaches his apostles about this radical
forgiveness, they respond with a spiritual-sounding but veiled
excuse. Basically they say, "Jesus, we're not ready to live that
graciously because you have not given us enough faith yet."
Jesus completely disagrees with their assessment. He tells a

parable that challenges them to overcome their resistant feelings and do their duty as followers to forgive. The slave in the story, after serving in the hot sun all day, would come in exhausted and hungry. He would not feel like doing more service. However, in a sense he had no choice because if he did what he wanted to, he would either be homeless or beaten. So, in spite of his feelings, he did his duty. This is what Jesus was saying to his followers: "Peter, James, John, and the rest of you guys, you need to do what I tell you to do. That is your Christian duty." Living graciously like our Lord is not a suggestion from our King. However, living dutifully is not all drudgery. This is what the teaching of the mulberry tree is all about. Mulberry trees are quite ordinary above ground. Below the ground they have an extensive and very stubborn root system. It is pretty much impossible to yank them out of the ground. What Jesus is saying here is this: "Even if your faith is small, if you will have the courage to do what I tell you, I will uproot big things out of your life."

Jenny had the courage to live out this radical grace. There were many times when she did not feel like loving her belligerent husband. She trusted God and consistently did what was right, and therefore God did the unexpected. He pulled up a stubborn tree. Her dutiful commitment led to a delightful marriage to a Christian husband. The whole church was blown away when he gave his life to Christ. Sadly, it doesn't always work out that way, but we never know unless we truly live out this teaching, not for a few weeks, but literally for a lifetime.

So husbands, are you like your Lord, a safe place of immense grace?

Husbands, love your wives and do not be embittered against them. (Colossians 3:19 NET)

The Holy Spirit through Paul specifically penned only one verse for all the Colossian husbands. Husbands, do not ever be resentful toward your wives. (Resentment is just a nicer word for bitterness.) One of the things that hurt our marriage for several years was my resentment toward my wife. My bitterness found its genesis in my self-righteous attitude toward her. I am so embarrassed to share this, but I really thought I was better than her. I have worked hard to overcome this sin in my heart, and gratitude has replaced resentment. Other than Jesus himself, Kelli is my greatest gift. I could boast and brag about my Proverbs 31 wife, but I think this book would end up being a thousand-page book. A while ago, although my wife didn't realize it, she hurt my feelings. As in previous years, I was strongly tempted to be resentful. The temptation would not subside, so I decided to pen a letter of gratitude. I wrote about all the reasons why I originally fell in love with her. That letter ended up being twelve pages long. By the time I finished it there wasn't a trace of bitterness within my heart, and to this day I still don't remember what she did that hurt me.

Oftentimes love is doing the exact opposite of what you feel. If a man has bitterness toward his wife, all the practical advice in the world won't do much good. For this reason, there are not a lot of practicals in this book. Instead, I am emphasizing the core issues of what makes relationships work. The question that transformed me in this area is this: is King Jesus ever resentful toward me? No, never, not even once in my forty-one years of Christianity has he been bitter toward me. Isn't that why grace is so amazing? I was a frustrated husband for many years, even though Jesus doesn't struggle with frustration toward me. I am trying now to love my wife the way he loves me, to be a little "throne of grace" that she can count on for help and encouragement (Hebrews 4:14–16, 10:10; Colossians 1:22).

Men should always treat their wives better than they deserve, because our spiritual husband always treats us that way. Over time, most wives will blossom under that kind of security-producing love. Frustrated men never create radiant wives. If you're frustrated like I was, it's probably because you're thinking about how your needs are not being met. I just can't see Jesus walking around brooding about his unmet needs. When his disciples were not there for him, he turned to God and continued to love his clueless friends. The key here is getting so deeply entrenched in Jesus that he becomes enough for you. If Jesus is enough, then you will not be thinking about what you don't have in your imperfect marriage. Contentment will replace frustration when you pursue Jesus as our brother Paul did (Philippians 3–4). There's no way to love like this without an ever-deepening relationship with Jesus Christ. Loving this way is beyond human strength. But, gentlemen, this is what we are called to, and it is the decision you made when you recited your marriage vows before God. Leadership is all about learning to love graciously.

PROMISE KEEPER

King Jesus is the ultimate promise keeper. Husbands, we made solemn vows before God and many witnesses on our wedding day. It's easy to make vows to your bride-to-be at your wedding ceremony. But promises at the altar are all about what you're going to do later, when the honeymoon is over. They are supposed to be conviction-filled promises of future love. "Kelli, I promise before God and these witnesses to love you...even when I don't feel like it...even when you hurt my feelings...even when you don't meet my needs...even if we have huge financial struggles...even if we have children with special needs...even if you develop a debilitating disease...even if we struggle mightily in our intimacy...even if you battle ongoing depression...even if the bad times seem to outweigh the good times." My friends, marriage is no joke. A man must come to the altar ready to make decisions like this in a clearheaded way. A man should count the cost before he proposes to a woman. If you are not ready, you will probably quit, because loving like Jesus is the hardest thing you will ever do. It is also the most fulfilling thing you will ever do, at least eventually.

Americans can be soft. I can say that because I'm from the United States. We are used to things being handed to us. Many things in life come easily to us. But that is hardly ever true in marriage. The typical male response when things get difficult in marriage is to become absorbed in our career, hobbies, or sports. It is an avoidance technique. And what we are avoiding are the vows we made to our bride. It is a common thought that women are more emotional than men. However, I don't think that is true. I believe men are just as moody as women are. Just because women may let their emotions bubble to the surface more often than men do, it doesn't mean that men are less emotional. Gentlemen, isn't it our feelings that often stop us from being selfless with our wives? And when we let our promises fall to the ground, isn't it because we just don't feel like fulfilling them?

One of the great signs of maturity is that we have learned to master our moods (1 Corinthians 9:24–27). I don't think a man is ready to be married unless he has progressed far in this arena. A man controlled by his feelings is still a boy, and women do not want to marry boys. In Titus chapter 2 men are given the challenge to be temperate, which means something like being even-tempered, consistent, and always refreshing. Even if our wife is running at 212° or -20° we husbands should do our best to remain at a calming 72°. We lived in Minneapolis for fourteen years. Every day I checked the weather channel because you never know what the weather will be like in Minnesota. When it comes to the climate of our love, our wives shouldn't feel like they're "living in Minnesota." The Titus 2 challenge is for men to be more like the temperate weather of San Diego. However, men, we are not supposed to deal with our feelings by suppressing them, but rather through learning to appropriately (without sinning) express them.

King Jesus was a man's man, primarily because he always kept his word. There isn't a promise that he hasn't fulfilled except for the ones that are yet in the future. But guaranteed, those promises will also be secured for us at the proper time. Even before the creation of the world, the promise was given for King Jesus to secure our salvation through the cross (Revelations

13:8). But from the beginning, Jesus our Bridegroom has had an extremely troubled relationship with his bride (Isaiah 65:2; Jeremiah 2:5; Ezekiel 16).

> "What can I do with you, Ephraim?
>> What can I do with you, Judah?
> Your love is like the morning mist,
>> like the early dew that disappears." (Hosea 6:4)

> I am jealous for you with a godly jealousy. I promised you to one husband, to Christ, so that I might present you as a pure virgin to him. But I am afraid that just as Eve was deceived by the serpent's cunning, your minds may somehow be led astray from your sincere and pure devotion to Christ. (2 Corinthians 11:2–3)

Yet through all the centuries of trouble, our covenant-keeping King has never let one of his vows drop to the ground. Instead of denying his bride, he died *for* her. Instead of divorcing this world, he found a way to remake it. And he is restoring this world to its original beauty not through intimidation, but through selfless sacrifice. Was it easy for Jesus to keep his covenant promises?

> Then he said to them, "My soul is overwhelmed with sorrow to the point of death. Stay here and keep watch with me."
> Going a little farther, he fell with his face to the ground and prayed, "My Father, if it is possible, may this cup be taken from me. Yet not as I will, but as you will." (Matthew 26:38–39)

Here we see the toughest man who ever walked the planet "overwhelmed with sorrow to the point of death." I don't even know what that desperate statement means. Was Jesus tempted to commit suicide? While on earth Jesus promised several times that he would die. In Gethsemane the seriousness of those vows was put to the test. Even though Jesus had total free will, he could not bear to disobey his Father or live without his bride. So he found the strength to die. Sometimes keeping your promises is a Gethsemane-like experience (Hebrews 5:7–9). Many men claim that they would die for their wife if some thug threatened her life. That may be true. However, what really proves a husband's love is his willingness to die daily for her (Luke 9:23; 2 Corinthians 5:14–15).

King Jesus was a relentless servant. I noted earlier that even in the age to come, he will still be serving us (Luke 12:37). Jesus has never been a part-time servant. Because God is love, God is a servant to the core of his being.

> Jesus called them together and said, "You know that the rulers of the Gentiles lord it over them, and their high officials exercise authority over them. Not so with you. Instead, whoever wants to become great among you must be your servant, and whoever wants to be first must be your slave— just as the Son of Man did not come to be served, but to serve, and to give his life as a ransom for many." (Matthew 20:25–28)

The Author of life gives us the best definition of leadership in the above passage. Do you want to become a great husband in the eyes of God? Then forget about yourself and enslave yourself to your wife's well-being (Deuteronomy 24:5). It doesn't matter if she notices or not; God will. If you are pouring yourself out so that she will change and bless you in return, you are loving her conditionally. Even if your wife never responds to your Christ-like love, you can still be an amazing image bearer. That is what you were created to be. Our spiritual Bridegroom has experienced that same struggle for thousands of years. Yet he keeps loving, serving, and pouring out his life in the hope that he can bless his bride. With Jesus, it's never about him, it's always about us. When I hear these lofty expectations that are placed upon us as husbands, my first reaction is, "There's no way!" It would be like someone calling me to be a first-string running back in the NFL. My thoughts would be, *"That would be so cool. But there is no way. I don't have what it takes. I'm sixty-two years old, 160 pounds and as slow as a three-legged turtle. Furthermore, I would get crushed. No way I can do that."* So in wisdom, I would turn that offer down.

Men, don't we do the same thing many times in this challenge to love like Jesus? So often we think of all the reasons why we can't, instead of all the reasons why we can. We remind ourselves of how we have been injured in the past, and why would it be any different in the future? So we ignore the offer. More than in any other sport, NFL players know they are going to be injured. Yet they still play with gusto. In our overmedicated modern world, we have found ingenious ways to avoid pain. Sometimes that is a good and helpful thing, but not when it comes to love. If you do not live by the wisdom of the cross, you will not experience the power of the cross (1 Corinthians 1–2). Your wife is worth dying for— at least Jesus seems to think so. God would not burden us with a challenge like this if he didn't also offer us the power to accomplish it. But we will not be blessed with that power if we sit on our hands making excuses. I will share some helpful practicals at the end of this chapter.

Now let's turn to the other great husband of Scripture, King Solomon.

SOLOMON

"Solomon a great husband? Are you kidding me?! Didn't that guy have 700 wives?" I can hear some of you at least thinking those words. No question about it, in the second half of his life Solomon completely caved in to the world. But at least for some time within his forty-year reign, he thrived spiritually. It appears that in his first years, when he was focused on building the temple, he did well. In the second half of his reign, he focused on building things for himself. That is always a recipe for disaster (Haggai 1).

> God gave Solomon wisdom and very great insight, and a
> breadth of understanding as measureless as the sand on the
> seashore. Solomon's wisdom was greater than the wisdom of all
> the people of the East, and greater than all the wisdom of Egypt.
> He was wiser than anyone else, including Ethan the Ezrahite—
> wiser than Heman, Kalkol and Darda, the sons of Mahol. And
> his fame spread to all the surrounding nations. He spoke three
> thousand proverbs and his songs numbered a thousand and
> five. He spoke about plant life, from the cedar of Lebanon to the
> hyssop that grows out of walls. He also spoke about animals and
> birds, reptiles and fish. From all nations people came to listen to
> Solomon's wisdom, sent by all the kings of the world, who had
> heard of his wisdom. (1 Kings 4:29–34)

There are three books in the Bible attributed to Solomon:
Proverbs, Ecclesiastes, and the *Song of Songs*. There are other authors who contributed to the book of Proverbs, and the
Song of Songs is co-authored with the Shulammite, the bride
in the Song. Jewish tradition says that Solomon wrote the *Song
of Songs* in his early years when he was excelling spiritually. He
penned his portion of the Proverbs in his middle years. During
his later, wandering years, he wrote Ecclesiastes. It is possible
that the Shulammite was his very first wife and that for some
time he enjoyed a monogamous relationship. However, we have
no proof of this. But it really doesn't matter, because the above
scripture says that God gave Solomon greater wisdom than anyone before or after him. The overall emphasis of these three
books has to do with relational wisdom. It is my strong convic-
tion that the greatest practical wisdom for making relationships
work is found in Solomon's writings. Isn't that what we read in
the above scripture? It is a tragedy that the wisdom found in
these books is so neglected. We should never dismiss the word
of God because the human author didn't continue to live by what
he wrote. It has always been God's intention that his new covenant people rely heavily not only on the New Testament, but also

the old (Matthew 13:52). The wisdom of Solomon can transform your life. It certainly has mine.

The greatest book ever written for future family leaders (husbands) is the book of Proverbs. While it is a book containing practical wisdom intended for everyone, the primary focus is for young men. We know this because the phrase "my son" is found in Proverbs at least forty times. If you want to learn to be an outstanding husband and father, the book of Proverbs is a great place to start.

The greatest book ever written specifically about marriage is the *Song of Songs*. Surprisingly, its first audience was women. The Song is unique in that it is the only book of the Bible in which the primary teacher is a woman. She teaches through her singing in 54 percent of the book, Solomon 34 percent, and the other singers 12 percent. It is certainly a book that all Christian women should be familiar with. Throughout history there have been more commentaries written on the *Song of Songs* than on any other book in the Bible. What the ancients were fascinated with, we moderns have almost completely ignored, to our own detriment. For the Song is the greatest book of wisdom ever written about human intimacy. This is true because it is the only book of romance we have that was written by God (2 Pet 1:20–21). The *Song of Songs* is just as inspired and therefore as authoritative as any of the other sixty-five books in the Bible.

Currently there are about 151,000 marriage books on Amazon. And there are another 190,000 on sex. The subjects of sex and marriage are huge in the minds of many people. I can't overstate this: we have only one book from God on marriage, and that little book of passionate poetry in the middle of your Bible outranks all those other books on Amazon. So if you are a married Christian and you're not educated in this book of marital wisdom, it might be a good time to trust what it says in the above passage. Solomon authored 1005 songs, all full of life-changing wisdom. So that our lives could be richly blessed, God saved for us the best of those songs. Admittedly, the Song is a difficult book, primarily because of the ancient poetry it contains. But with a little help, you can excavate rich truths about your intimacy with your spouse and God.

Solomon was an amazing husband for a while. The Shulammite poetically describes him in glowing terms:

> Let him kiss me with the kisses of his mouth—
>   for your love is more delightful than wine.
>   (Song of Songs 1:2)

His love makes her drunk, giddy, silly, and lightheaded!

> My beloved is to me a cluster of henna blossoms
>   from the vineyards of En Gedi. (Song of Songs 1:14)

En Gedi is an oasis surrounded by harsh desert. Finding a cool oasis with vineyards while traveling through the desert would be a most refreshing experience. With this beautiful metaphor she is saying, "He encourages my soul; life is like a scorching desert until I come home to be with my husband."

> Listen! My beloved!
>   Look! Here he comes,
> leaping across the mountains,
>   bounding over the hills. (Song of Songs 2:8)

This metaphor is obvious: he is my superman, and I feel safe with him.

What was it about Solomon's love that refreshed her and made her feel safe and drunk with love? Here are just a few things. (This list will not be exhaustive, because that would take a commentary on the entire Song).

Solomon was a great listener and therefore was remarkably in tune to his wife's heartfelt needs. The challenge to listen is found in the Bible at least 412 times, probably because there is a shortage of great listeners among us. I know that I for many years was a poor listener, especially with my bride. Husbands, undistracted listening may be the number one activity that shows that you treasure your wife. Listening to her with your heart fully engaged is a necessity for my wife and yours. Solomon was an expert listener.

> O my dove, in the clefts of the rock,
>> in the crannies of the cliff,
> let me see your face,
>> let me hear your voice,
> for your voice is sweet,
>> and your face is lovely.
> Catch the foxes for us,
>> the little foxes
> that spoil the vineyards,
>> for our vineyards are in blossom.
>> (Song of Songs 2:14–15 ESV)

These two little verses are pregnant with life-changing relational wisdom. Let's do a little study. First, Solomon understands that his wife is a dove, not an armadillo. It is one of his favorite nicknames for her. He understands that she is pure, innocent, and easily hurt, like a dove. Because of this, he treats her with great kindness. Kind men are treasures. Solomon notices that something is troubling her because metaphorically she is hiding out of reach on the side of a cliff. She seems emotionally distant. So he initiates a conversation in an attempt to find out what is bothering her. He knows that he cannot just guess at these things. Out of concern, he asks as many love-laced questions as needed to discover why she's feeling so insecure. Her "voice is sweet," so he loves connecting with her through meaningful conversations. Her insecurities cause him to be compassionate, not irritated. He doesn't look down his kingly nose because of the things she feels anxious about. I have learned that things that

don't bother me at all often trouble my wife deeply. If I am con-
descending toward her in any way, she will remain distant from
me "up in the cliffs." Solomon is the king of an entire country,
yet he takes the time to listen. He notices that some little foxes
have wandered into their garden. He does the very opposite of
Adam (Genesis 3) and assertively deals with the little critters
that could ruin their Edenic love. Solomon was the kind of husband who, if his wife requested they see a counselor, would be
eager about that proposal. He might be the first to suggest it.
A rare man indeed. The health of their relationship was of the
utmost importance to him. Here's a practical that has helped
me: husbands, watch how your wife's girlfriends listen to her.
I noticed that when she is sharing her heart, they always give
their undivided attention, complete with much empathy. Most of
us know how to do this. When you were dating, none of your fiancé's words dropped to the ground. It is one of the reasons why
she fell in love with you. Since the leader of an entire country
had time to listen to his wife, I think I do too. A woman married
to this kind of man will "fly down from the cliffs" to be close to
him. Solomon and his wife were best friends because of his sen-
sitivity (Song of Songs 5:16).

Another reason that Solomon was a husband worthy of imitation is his constant and convincing encouragements.

> How beautiful you are, my darling!
>> Oh, how beautiful!
>> Your eyes are doves. (Song of Songs 1:15)

> Like a lily among thorns
>> is my darling among the young women.
>>> (Song of Songs 2:2)

> How beautiful you are, my darling!
>> Oh, how beautiful!
>> Your eyes behind your veil are doves.

Your hair is like a flock of goats
  descending from the hills of Gilead. (Song of Songs 4:1)

You are altogether beautiful, my darling;
  there is no flaw in you. (Song of Songs 4:7)

How beautiful your sandaled feet,
  O prince's daughter!
Your graceful legs are like jewels,
  the work of an artist's hands. (Song of Songs 7:1)

Many years ago the first thing I noticed about the Song was Solomon's frequent, persuasive encouragements. It seems that he was willing to follow King Lemuel's sage advice from the Proverbs:

Her children arise and call her blessed;
  her husband also, and he praises her:
"Many women do noble things,
  but you surpass them all."
Charm is deceptive, and beauty is fleeting;
  but a woman who fears the LORD is to be praised.
Honor her for all that her hands have done,
  and let her works bring her praise at the city gate.
  (Proverbs 31:28–31)

Through my study of the wisdom literature, I have a little different take on Proverbs 31. Since the book of Proverbs was primarily written for men, it stands to reason that this chapter is as much of a challenge for husbands as it is for wives. Proverbs 31 reveals how a man ought to think about and treat his wife. It challenges husbands to profusely express appreciation for the love warrior who relentlessly serves the entire family and others. It is very instructive to me that sexual intimacy is not even mentioned. Not because it is unimportant, but rather because we men tend to overemphasize that area of life. Proverbs 31 has schooled me in being forever thankful for *all* that my wife does. Here is a thought-provoking fact: even to this day, committed Jewish men recite from memory Proverbs 31:10–31 to their wives at the beginning of every Sabbath. This is done not as a corrective, but in glowing gratitude for her constant service. Sons watching their father adore their wives in such a manner learn how to treat their future wife. Daughters are inspired to be like their mother, and this fortunate woman is encouraged to continue her untiring service. The Hebrew language in Proverbs 31 is lofty indeed. It literally is the kind of language that you would use to describe a warrior who has saved an entire country through his bravery. It is a tragedy how the modern world views a woman who lays down her life for her husband and children. I think most men desire to have a Proverbs 31 woman. This highly instructive passage teaches men how to inspire one.

I remember not long ago getting together with a young couple who were having some huge marital problems. The husband was constantly complaining about his wife's way of taking care of the home. As I entered their house, I certainly saw what he was concerned about. The place was a mess. After listening intently for some time, I turned to him with a loving but fiery correction about his negativity. As soon as he said that he was sorry, even before I left, she got up and started to clean the house. Women are never motivated by frustration, negativity, or a complaining spirit. They are inspired by encouragement and the self-less service of their husbands. When a woman lives within an atmosphere of appreciation, then when a correction is needed, she will usually respond positively. When I left, they were both laughing and cleaning the house together.

Our lives would be much more fulfilling if we were more serious about following the challenges contained within the Bible. Husbands, it certainly would be a fine practice to encourage our wives through Proverbs 31 each week. Every household has an atmosphere to it, a mood or aroma. So does every relationship.

Some people enter a room and everybody brightens up. Another person comes through the door and everybody tenses up. When Solomon came home, the fragrance of his spirit brought joy to his wife. He was her greatest fan, and she knew it. Have you ever heard the saying, "If momma ain't happy, ain't nobody happy"? A Christian household should never buy into that thinking. Mom's sour emotions should not lead the family. Husbands, that's our job. It is our God-given responsibility to create an encouraging atmosphere within our homes. Solomon's convincing praises transformed the Shulammite. Her transformation from insecurity to radiance is one of the biggest themes in the Song. That brings up the question, why were his encouragements so transforming? As you read this 3000-year-old poetry you can tell this man is completely enamored with his wife. The reason she became so secure was because she could tell he was so convinced that she was amazing in every way. Because he was convinced, he was convincing. About a decade ago, that is what fundamentally changed within my soul. I finally realized how amazing my wife truly is. So now I encourage her not so much because I'm supposed to; rather, I just can't help myself. This heart change within me began with seeing my wife the way God does.

> Dark am I, yet lovely,
>   daughters of Jerusalem,
> dark like the tents of Kedar,
>   like the tent curtains of Solomon.
> Do not stare at me because I am dark,
>   because I am darkened by the sun.
> My mother's sons were angry with me
>   and made me take care of the vineyards;
> my own vineyard I had to neglect. (Song of Songs 1:5–6)

At the beginning of their relationship, she is struggling with insecurity. The other women in Jerusalem stare at her thinking, *"Wow, what does the king see in her!"* In those days, a tan was considered a major beauty flaw. You see, Solomon fell in love with the most unlikely woman, a slave girl from one of his northern vineyards. Most assuredly King Solomon could have any woman he desired (sadly, that did happen later). Yet he falls for this one, whom most would consider an ugly duckling. He spotted her in the fields with her dirty, matted hair and loose-fitting clothing and fell in love with her. No spa treatments, no makeup, no stylish hairdo, no body-trimming workouts, no immodest curve-revealing clothing, just a woman with a beautiful, serving character. That must be what he fell in love with. Maybe he noticed how kind she was to the other workers. Or possibly he just saw how hard she worked in the hot sun. I'm not a big quote person. Why be blown away by what people say when we have the word of God? However, I do love this quote that I came upon (please note: despite my research, I have not been able to identify who A.B. is).

You don't fall in love with a body, you fall in love with a soul. And once in love with a soul, everything about that body becomes beautiful. – A.B.

Just as Jesus sees past our sin, Solomon could see the beauty underneath her unkempt appearance. Her sun-darkened skin didn't turn the king away. Like Solomon, King Jesus retrieves the beauty deep inside of us through his adoring love. This is the narrative behind this little book of poetry: it is the whole Bible story in miniature. The King of kings falls in love with the most unworthy bride, and his gracious love transforms her into radiance (Ephesians 5:25–27).

The Shulammite enters Jerusalem under the stares of critical women but later is praised by those same women as the most beautiful queen (Song of Songs 6:8–10). A Christ-like husband can have that kind of influence on a goodhearted woman. Selfless love can remake people. Their love was based on deeper things than the beauty standards of their culture. After all, what does the world know about what is truly beautiful? Not much! This was a big reason why Solomon's love was so intoxicating.

The Saindon family are animal lovers. When we lived in Los Angeles we had so many pets that our backyard was seen as the neighborhood petting zoo. We had ferrets, snakes, toads, frogs, turtles, a bearded dragon, birds, cats, hamsters, and as many as twenty-one guinea pigs. We are especially dog lovers, so throughout the years we have rescued six dogs. Currently, my wife and I have a cute little dog named Charlie. She is a strange combination of a rat terrier (courageous far beyond their size), a chow (ferocious "lion dogs"), and a chihuahua (shivering fur-balls of insecurity). Surprisingly, she is a delightful and loving puppy dog. Her only flaw is that whenever she sees another dog, regardless of its size, she turns into a raging werewolf, all thirty-two pounds of her. So for us, the dog park is off limits. She has been our most trainable dog except in that one area. She has made it clear to us that she will not stop picking fights with other dogs. Sadly, men and women often do the same thing, especially in the area of intimacy, to their own detriment. There are certain areas that we are just too insecure about to be trained in. We let our "inner chihuahua" take over. Then, in defense, to camouflage our insecurities we act like a combination of a rat terrier and a chow. At least that's how Charlie and some people deal with things like that.

Long before Charlie, we rescued another dog for our youngest daughter. Sadie is the most sensitive, caring person you would ever want to meet. So when we went to the pound, she found the dog that no one else would ever choose for adoption. She named him Chopper. I called him Train Wreck because he looked like he had had a head-on collision with a freight train. And no, he was not one of those dogs that was so ugly he was cute. He was just ugly. Chopper came to us with a lot of baggage. It was immediately obvious to us that he had been severely abused in his past. His little traumatized soul caused him to run for cover anytime anyone entered our home. Even a sneeze would send him running. We tried our best to love him out of his dysfunctional past, but nothing we did seemed to help. One day, for no apparent reason, he ran out of our yard and bit one of our neighbors. The girl's father was livid, and Train Wreck was back at the pound the next day. For whatever reasons, we were unable to transform him out of his trauma.

> What can I say for you?
>   With what can I compare you,
>   Daughter Jerusalem?
> To what can I liken you,
>   that I may comfort you,
>   Virgin Daughter Zion?
> Your wound is as deep as the sea.
>   Who can heal you?
>
> The visions of your prophets
>   were false and worthless;
> they did not expose your sin
>   to ward off your captivity.
> The prophecies they gave you
>   were false and misleading. (Lamentations 2:13–14)

Chopper's wounds were "as deep as the sea." This is also true of many people. Everyone has baggage. Even if you have only sinned once in your life (no such person), or have only been sinned against on one occasion (no such person), you have baggage. Some have existed in the realm of trauma for so long that they don't even know what it feels like to have healthy thoughts about God, themselves, or others. They may genuinely love God and people, but their hurts have defined in their minds who God is and who people and they themselves are. They view everything through a distorted lens. For many of us, what we run after in life is what we believe will fill up the hole in our soul. The virgin daughter Zion wasn't healed, because she relied on false healers. The only one who can truly heal your soul is the one who created it. All too often, we avoid going to the Great Physician because we know we are not going to like his diagnosis or his prescriptions. So we are content to call on anemic healers who will cover up our symptoms instead of curing the core issues within our souls. The results are that we walk around half healed and scared to death of the deepest forms of intimacy. This was our frustrating story. Whenever Kelli and I tried to get close, my baggage bumped into hers, so instead of unbridled joy there was tension. We are in a much better place now, but we both still have some baggage. We always will in this life to some degree. Only in the next life will we enjoy complete healing. We must learn to be content with that. However, we can experience great progress in this area if we wholeheartedly believe and follow what Dr. Jesus says.

The *Song of Songs* is a book about healing and transformation. Because Solomon was such a gracious husband, God was able to use his love to bring much healing into his wife's life. Let's do a little study of *Song of Songs* 4.

He

How beautiful you are, my darling!
Oh, how beautiful!
Your eyes behind your veil are doves.
Your hair is like a flock of goats
descending from the hills of Gilead.
Your teeth are like a flock of sheep just shorn,
coming up from the washing.
Each has its twin;
not one of them is alone.
Your lips are like a scarlet ribbon;
your mouth is lovely.
Your temples behind your veil

are like the halves of a pomegranate.
Your neck is like the tower of David,
    built with courses of stone;
on it hang a thousand shields,
    all of them shields of warriors.
Your breasts are like two fawns,
    like twin fawns of a gazelle
      that browse among the lilies.
Until the day breaks
    and the shadows flee,
I will go to the mountain of myrrh
    and to the hill of incense.
You are altogether beautiful, my darling;
    there is no flaw in you.

Come with me from Lebanon, my bride,
    come with me from Lebanon.
Descend from the crest of Amana,
    from the top of Senir, the summit of Hermon,
from the lions' dens
    and the mountain haunts of leopards.
You have stolen my heart, my sister, my bride;
    you have stolen my heart
with one glance of your eyes,
    with one jewel of your necklace.
How delightful is your love, my sister, my bride!
    How much more pleasing is your love than wine,
and the fragrance of your perfume
    more than any spice!
Your lips drop sweetness as the honeycomb, my bride;
    milk and honey are under your tongue.
The fragrance of your garments

is like the fragrance of Lebanon.
You are a garden locked up, my sister, my bride;
    you are a spring enclosed, a sealed fountain.
Your plants are an orchard of pomegranates
    with choice fruits,
    with henna and nard,
    nard and saffron,
    calamus and cinnamon,
    with every kind of incense tree,
    with myrrh and aloes
    and all the finest spices.
You are a garden fountain,
    a well of flowing water
    streaming down from Lebanon.

She

Awake, north wind,
    and come, south wind!
Blow on my garden,
    that its fragrance may spread everywhere.
Let my beloved come into his garden
    and taste its choice fruits.

He

I have come into my garden, my sister, my bride;
    I have gathered my myrrh with my spice.
I have eaten my honeycomb and my honey;
    I have drunk my wine and my milk.

Friends

Eat, friends, and drink;
    drink your fill of love. (Song of Songs 4:1–5:1)

It is pretty crazy how the *Song of Songs* begins. The young bride-to-be is aching for intimacy with the King she has fallen in love with. She is not longing for a grandma kiss, but rather a steamy and passionate rendezvous. She is wanting to get married and get on with the honeymoon. In chapter three of the Song they are married. Chapter four is a poetic God-endorsed description of their honeymoon. In chapter one it appears that the Shulammite has little baggage. She doesn't appear to be anxious about intimacy. However, in chapter four we see a much different story. It appears that her brothers had dealt with her harshly, and her wounded soul reveals itself on their wedding night (Song of Songs 1:5–6). The baggage always comes out when we feel most vulnerable, and there is nothing more vulnerable than sexual intimacy. The passionate woman of chapter one has suddenly become tense, insecure, even sex averse. This abused woman has some major luggage that they must deal with together.

Before we dive any further into this, I want to share something about ancient poetry. Most theologians believe that this is the honeymoon night, and that is probably true. However, it would be a mistake to limit it to only one night or one week. Chronology means little in Hebrew poetry. This could be the honeymoon night, or it could be a whole season at the beginning of their marriage. In other words, it could be a picture of their first few months or even years together. It's important to understand that.

How do we know that she is struggling with major insecurities? Because in Song of Songs 4:12 it says that she is all locked up. Earlier, in verse 8, it tells us why. The metaphors in this poetry are beautiful and practical. Solomon is questioning why his wife is distant. He states that she is on the top of three different mountains at the same time, obviously a metaphor because that physically couldn't be true. "Sweetheart, you seem so far away," is what he is saying to his bride. Her anxieties are explained by the fact that there are metaphorical lions and leopards roaming around in her head. She doesn't feel safe, so it is nearly impossible for her to relax in this ultra-vulnerable moment. She's getting naked and she does not feel comfortable with that. Remember, we husbands were created to be a safe place for our wives. If you were walking through the tall African grass and you heard the rustling of lions just a few yards away, you would not be able to relax. Even if you were well armed, you would not be able to enjoy your stroll in the savanna. You would be completely on edge. In a sense, we husbands need to learn how to become lion tamers.

I am ashamed to reveal this, but I used to be very irritated at the things my wife often felt anxious about, which just meant that I was another lion lurking in her head. A few years ago, I realized that I needed to stop looking at her weaknesses as her problems but rather as our challenges to be tackled together. I also needed to realize that I had just as many weaknesses as she does, if not more. When we were married, her baggage became mine and mine became hers. As a spouse, you can be an agent of healing or of hurt. Now as an older and hopefully wiser husband, I consider it a great privilege to help my wife with her luggage, whether that be at the airport or in life. I pray every single day that I can be a safe place for this amazing woman that God has given me.

There were many things that Solomon's wife could have been troubled about. Here is a possible list of the lions that were prowling around in her head.

1. She had probably lived in Lebanon all her life. Now she's in Jerusalem, the city of David, the city of God. Everything is new and different. Nothing is familiar. All her comforting routines have disappeared. She misses her friends and especially her mom. The only person she knows is the king. Big transitions can create much anxiety.

2. She feels completely unworthy to be married to the king. What could he possibly see in her? Kings don't marry slaves. A few weeks ago, she was a servant girl living an impoverished life. Now she is married to the most influential man on the planet. Is this real? And now I am in the king's bedroom. In a few moments he's going to see me completely naked. Once he really knows me, will he still be in love with me? Will he be disappointed? All of a sudden, the critical stares of the jealous women of Jerusalem (Song of Songs 1:5–6) are at the forefront of her mind. The lions and leopards are chewing on her soul. They are eating up her confidence and swallowing her security. Why does that happen in these vulnerable settings? Why does what other people wrongly think of us bubble up from our memory banks in our most intimate moments? Shame is the ferocious feline that creates these overwhelming

insecurities. Shame was the very first consequence of the very first sin (Genesis 3). In some ways it is the ugly result of any sin. Why did Adam and Eve feel so insecure after they ate the forbidden fruit? It seems to me that the beginning of their shame was their critical thoughts of God. The devil painted unworthy pictures of their selfless Creator, and they believed it. Criticism was the catalyst of the first sin. If you will believe critical things about our holy God, I know you will have critical thoughts of me. Lesser thoughts of our Creator will always create lesser thoughts about his creatures. This is how intimacy-killing shame was born. Shame severely damages self-esteem, and a low self-esteem shuts the door on intoxicating intimacy. In *Song of Songs* chapter one the bride was ready to go, but now she is frozen because of her insecurities.

3. Most likely the largest of the lions munching on her soul was her dysfunctional history. Her brothers had abused her. Out of bitterness, it appears, they made her do their work in the fields. We do not know where her father or mother were in all this. We only know that she was not accustomed to being treated with kindness, especially by men. In the last few weeks or months a completely different kind of man had entered her life. She had never met anyone like him, and he completely swept her off her feet. *Is this too good to be true? Did I say yes too quickly? But you don't say no to the king. That was not even an option. Did I just say yes to improve my situation? Are my motives pure? Was I just tired of being a slave? After we are married for a few weeks, is he going to change and become like the other men in my life?* She most certainly had seen other people begin marriage in a great way and then after a while their relationship ended up destroyed. *All*

*these nice things that he has said, are they real? Or
does he just want some great sex? And if I don't give
him that, is he going to toss me to the side? After all, he
can have any woman he wants.* The lions and leopards
are roaring, and she is scared to death. Anxiety and
bedroom love do not mix well. So she retreats up into
a metaphorical mountain and hides away in the cliffs.
She is all locked up.

Men do the same thing in a different way. Many times when
we are having a tense conversation with our wife and we give
her the silent treatment, we are just hiding away in our imaginary mountain. We are jammed up emotionally and experience
a strange form of "lockjaw." Gentlemen, as you read this, do not
let yourself struggle with some kind of relational self-righteous-
ness. Men have just as many worries and hang-ups as the more
tender gender. Men fret about whether they are successful, and
women worry about whether they are desirable. Sounds similar,
doesn't it? We both worry about whether we are enough.

Too often it is our insecurities that determine our focus, not
God. If a husband feels unsuccessful, he will throw himself into
his work. Traditionally, if a wife felt insecure about her role in
marriage, she would absorb herself in her children. However, in
recent times that has changed. Now more and more women are
also becoming highly involved in their careers. We all desperately want to feel good about ourselves, and there is nothing wrong
with that. But the only way to accomplish it is to humbly listen
to God and follow his plan for our lives. If you are married, the
number one priority in your life in pleasing God is to love your
spouse. Your marriage is not the only thing on your God-list, but
it is the first. To get a taste of the abundant life that Jesus promises, it is vital that we let God write our list of priorities. The Spirit
longs to intoxicate us with joy, but his hands are tied if we, out
of ignorance or stubbornness, keep calling the shots. Especially
when it comes to something as important as marriage.

Kelli and I experienced many years of frustration because we didn't know how God viewed marriage. That was my fault, for two reasons. First, I am the husband, the God-appointed leader. Second, I am a preacher called to know and follow God's word. All husbands are responsible for knowing God's plan for marriage, but because I am an evangelist I feel I am doubly responsible. How can you lead if you don't even know where you're going? We go to school to be a carpenter, a doctor, an engineer, or a plumber. Yet my preparation for marriage amounted to one twelve-minute talk with another minister. I do not blame my friend, because the responsibility is mainly mine. What if your minister doesn't do his job? That does not make you innocent of ignorance, especially with all the biblical resources we have available to us in this modern age. When it comes to difficulty, it seems to me that marriage is on the same level as brain surgery. We would never let an unschooled brain surgeon cut into our skull. And we should never "let" uninstructed people get married. We can't stop people from getting married, of course, but we can educate them if they are willing. That is one of the chief reasons I decided to write this book.

How does King Solomon, this relational expert, handle his wife's timidity, whether it was on their honeymoon night or it was a whole season at the beginning of their marriage? Every husband I am aware of has been full of God-approved anticipation of their honeymoon. How the King handles this is most educational. There is no hint of disappointment, frustration, or impatience. He is aware of the lions, and he knows that it will take a lot to quiet their roars. Solomon was in tune with the atmosphere of his wife's inner being. The condition of her soul was more important than his pleasure. To him, sex was not about his gratification, but about their connection. He didn't separate emotional and sexual intimacy. It truly is amazing how this incredibly wise man helps his wife feel safe in the most vulnerable moment of her life. I have a little exercise for you. Go back and read *Song of Songs* chapter four. There is a little word in the chapter that is repeated over and over, especially in the New International Version. What little word is it and what does it mean?

King Solomon makes his new wife feel secure by letting her know in numerous ways that she is his. That they are one. The little word "my" is repeated at least twenty times. He understands that marriage is a lifelong covenant. He reassures her that he understands that marriage is all about belonging to one another. As important as sexual intimacy is, marriage is all about a covenant between two souls. His most desperate concern is for her soul, and because of that she eventually responds with her body (Song of Songs 4:12–5:1). Let me remind you that we cannot saddle this poetry with time limits. Did it take a few minutes for her to respond? Or weeks, months, or even years?

Husbands, we especially need to be prepared to selflessly love our covenant partner if they have been abused in any way. Whether it be verbal, physical, or sexual abuse, harsh treatment deeply traumatizes the soul of the more tender gender. Usually the inner lions of such a woman will be the most ferocious during bedroom love. If you are selfish in the bedroom, you are only going to bring more hurt and insecurity to the soul of your wife. As a Christian leader I was reasonably good at carrying my cross around every day. But when it came time for some intimacy with Kelli, I often left Jesus' cross of self-denial outside our bedroom door. From either husband or wife, selfishness is one of the biggest intimacy killers. Because of what I have learned from the *Song of Songs*, I am trying hard to be a safe place for the soul of my wife. Not an easy task, to be a caregiver along with God for the soul of another. Solomon understood what Adam apparently forgot, that the real garden he was called to protect was his wife. This is why he refers to her in the poetry as "a garden" (Song of Songs 4:12). Mistakenly, some theologians teach that her garden is her vagina. They teach that when she invites him into her garden (Song of Songs 4:16), she is requesting intercourse. I think that is only partially true. A man can enter a woman but not be in her garden (her soul, her whole being). Sadly, men pay for that kind of stuff all the time. The reason that kind of sex is so disappointing is because you enter a body but not the soul. God did not create sex only for physical pleasure, and if we treat it that way, we ruin it. Sex was created by God to glue husband and wife together. From the get-go, Solomon reveals that he is concerned about his wife's inner garden.

> How beautiful you are, my darling!
>> Oh, how beautiful!
>> Your eyes behind your veil are doves.
> Your hair is like a flock of goats
>> descending from the hills of Gilead. (Song of Songs 4:1)

On their wedding night and throughout their life together, he looks into her soul before he gazes upon her body. He starts with her eyes because they are the windows into her inner being, her beautiful garden. It's as if he wants to make sure that her soul is in good shape, healthy, strong, and secure, before progressing. Isn't that why he notices that she's feeling distant and insecure? So it appears that he slows things way down to help her deal with those feisty felines. He is not about to make love when they are emotionally distant, because that wouldn't be making love. The momentary glances from her soul through her eyes drive him crazy (Song of Songs 4:9). But brief eye contact is a sign of great insecurity, and he knows it. He wisely sees this as a sign that everything is not OK in her garden. A lack of eye contact is the surest sign of soul trouble. It reveals that there are some critters in the garden. So, gentlemen, let's become experts at looking into the souls of our brides. Only then will they feel safe. Being willing to take time for sex but not conversation was one of the biggest mistakes I made as a younger husband. Sexual touching should be preceded by sincere talking, which also means undistracted listening. Don't assume you understand what kind of lion or leopard is roaring at your wife. Remember, one of the greatest keys for building intimacy with your wife is this: whatever is most important to her should be intensely important to you. Blowing off her concerns because they don't cause you anxiety is self-centered. It never ceases to amaze me that some husbands disregard their wife's worries because they seem insignificant, yet when their wife is not concerned about the things on her husband's heart, they wonder how she can be so selfish. "Hey, Joe, she's just following your lead," is my usual response.

If your wife has any kind of hurt in her past, you as her loving husband need to be prepared to be very patient. Healing from deep wounds usually takes a long time. Furthermore, for whatever reasons, some heal up more quickly than others. I have always been pretty healthy throughout my sixty-two years of living. A few years ago I passed some kidney stones (razor-sharp ninja star-like boulders). Other than that excruciating experience, I haven't had many struggles with my health. At least not until recently. In the last two years I've had four surgeries that included some torturously slow and frustrating healing. Even now I can only be on my feet for two hours at a time. Standing is a struggle and sitting is the worst. I have to be on my back for a good portion of each day to help with pain management and other issues. For a guy who likes to work hard in ministry, it has been a major challenge. During one of my post-op appointments, my doctor told me that the reason it had been going so slowly was because my healing would be "violent." That is the exact word he used. Some parts of the body heal more easily and quickly than other parts. This is also true in the body of Christ. I have learned to be patient and pamper that area of my body that has been traumatized. I am not talking about sentimentality, but rather empathy and compassion. Men tend to be weaker in those areas than women. However, if you are married to a woman who has a hurt-filled history, it is vital that you learn to be an expert in sympathy. Jesus is, and we are called to love just like he does.

I am convinced that it is more difficult to be a woman than

a man. That is why women are referred to in 1 Peter 3:7 as the "weaker partner." That phrase has nothing to do with physical, emotional, spiritual, or intellectual weakness. That doesn't make sense with the context of the passage, which says:

> Slaves, in reverent fear of God submit yourselves to your masters, not only to those who are good and considerate, but also to those who are harsh. For it is commendable if someone bears up under the pain of unjust suffering because they are conscious of God. But how is it to your credit if you receive a beating for doing wrong and endure it? But if you suffer for doing good and you endure it, this is commendable before God. To this you were called, because Christ suffered for you, leaving you an example, that you should follow in his steps.
> "He committed no sin,
> and no deceit was found in his mouth."
> When they hurled their insults at him, he did not retaliate; when he suffered, he made no threats. Instead, he entrusted himself to him who judges justly. "He himself bore our sins" in his body on the cross, so that we might die to sins and live for righteousness; "by his wounds you have been healed." For "you were like sheep going astray," but now you have returned to the Shepherd and Overseer of your souls.
> Wives, in the same way submit yourselves to your own husbands so that, if any of them do not believe the word, they may be won over without words by the behavior of their wives, when they see the purity and reverence of your lives. Your beauty should not come from outward adornment, such as elaborate hairstyles and the wearing of gold jewelry or fine clothes. Rather, it should be that of your inner self, the unfading beauty of a gentle and quiet spirit, which is of great worth in God's sight. For this is the way the holy women of the past who put their hope in God used to adorn themselves. They submitted themselves to their own husbands, like Sarah, who obeyed Abraham and called him her lord. You are her daughters if you do what is right and do not

give way to fear.

Husbands, in the same way be considerate as you live with your wives, and treat them with respect as the weaker partner and as heirs with you of the gracious gift of life, so that nothing will hinder your prayers. (1 Peter 2:18–3:7)

Like the slave (1 Peter 2:18–20), like Jesus (1 Peter 2:21–25), and like Sarah (1 Peter 3:5–6), she is in a more vulnerable life situation because of who is over her. My wife is "weaker" because she is under my authority. And last time I checked, I'm still a struggling sinner like everyone else. Too often people have concluded this to be a chauvinistic passage, when in truth, it is a challenge to husbands. Don't be like the harsh slave owner or even Abraham when he was thinking about his own safety much more than his wife's (Genesis 12, 20). In other words, Kelli is weaker when I am weaker in Jesus. So, yes, it is more difficult for our wives.

Recently, I decided to do something a little strange. For a day, I tried to pretend I was a woman. With what I have learned over the last thirty-five years of marriage and the last few years of reading many books authored by women, I tried to think like a typical wife. I wanted to know what it would feel like to be my wife. I am confident that my experiment fell short, but I think it did help me understand a few things.

As I was getting ready to go to the store to get some milk and eggs, I turned on the TV. I noticed that on every commercial selling man stuff there was some "hot chick" advertising the you-gotta-have-this product. I knew that was going to happen, but I wanted to try to process these things like a woman. "If I have to look like that to be considered hot, then maybe I'm not so hot." During the half hour that I was getting ready, I experienced this several times. Maybe I should have listened to a podcast instead. On the way to the store there were at least three beautiful billboard ladies shaking their skinny fingers at me with the same message. "You're not tall enough, skinny enough, busty enough, or pretty enough to be enough." At the store, I noticed that the ordinary women were looking at the beautiful women more than men were, comparing, assessing, scrutinizing, and judging themselves according to the pathetic standards of this shallow age. Once I got my eggs and milk, I was accosted by the slender, self-righteous *Cosmo* girl on the magazine rack. She told me that I was "not sexy enough!" When I turned away from the magazine mean girls, I couldn't help but notice the workout chick in front of me in line. Even though she had three young children, she apparently had a lot more time on her hands than I did. She was chiseled, shapely, and hard as a rock. It was like she had a neon sign on her back, flashing "What's your excuse?... What's your excuse?... What's your excuse?" On my way home, I was once again rebuked by the billboard beauties. They wanted to make sure that I got the message. "Face it, lady, you are just ordinary and not very desirable!" At that moment I pretended I got a text from my imaginary husband, "Hey sweetheart, honey bunny, my sweet cuddle-muffin, do you want to have a date tonight?" Ugh... "Hmmm...well...sure, I guess." My poor out-of-touch husband was hurt because I wasn't enthusiastic, but it was only because I felt so ugly, not because I didn't love him.

Helping men stay pure is not the only reason the Bible says that women should dress modestly. It also protects women from what I just described. In the world, those conservative days are gone. Probably for good. The world thinks that the dress standards in the Bible are completely out of date and unnecessary. It is shocking to see how some people dress even at church. The standards of the world are always trying to slither into the church fellowship. Men are battling with the temptation to lust and women are battling with the temptation to be insecure—during communion. This should not be (1 Timothy 2:9–10).

I think I'm only now beginning to understand how the shallow standards of this world have crushed the souls of our wives. The constant and negative voice that they hear was illustrated in my funny little exercise, that when you really think about it wasn't all that funny. The part of the brain responsible for recognizing errors and flaws is larger in the female brain. This makes women more prone to insecurity, low self-esteem, and criticalness of themselves and others.

Some believe it starts all the way back when a little girl gets her first Barbie doll. Isn't that where many of the eating disorders come from, out-of-control insecurities? Isn't that why millions are spent and facelifts, boob jobs, and wrinkle creams? I think my wife's wrinkles are gorgeous. She doesn't like them so much, but I think they give testimony to a relentless love warrior who has laid down her life for decades. The world keeps trying to tell her that her wrinkles are a flaw that needs to be fixed. It is my job to try to outshout the world and convince her that she's more beautiful than ever. If you study the *Song of Songs* or Proverbs 31, you get the right picture of how a husband is to treat his wife. Let's ponder on a few other proverbs.

> The tongue has the power of life and death,
>> and those who love it will eat its fruit. (Proverbs 18:21)

The tongue has great power. It can create life or death. It is especially destructive if it is misused by a husband. An undeserved curse from the man who vowed to love you is crushing.

> Like a fluttering sparrow or a darting swallow,
>> an undeserved curse does not come to rest. (Proverbs 26:2)

> The soothing tongue is a tree of life,
>> but a perverse tongue crushes the spirit. (Proverbs 15:4)

> The words of the reckless pierce like swords,
>> but the tongue of the wise brings healing. (Proverbs 12:18)

Sometimes the genesis of a man's negativity is his worldly mindset. He's educated more by the current standards than by the word of God. The very first man, Adam, did not have this problem. The only standards that existed were God's. Hollywood and all its goofiness did not exist yet. I have a degree in art from Eastern Illinois University. Throughout history there have been countless paintings of the very first couple. Eve was always painted according to the beauty standards of the age in which the artist lived. Yet we don't really know what she looked like. However she looked, Adam was mesmerized and responded with the very first love song.

The man said,

"This is now bone of my bones
  and flesh of my flesh;
she shall be called 'woman,'
  for she was taken out of man."

That is why a man leaves his father and mother and is united to his wife, and they become one flesh.

Adam and his wife were both naked, and they felt no shame. (Genesis 2:23–25)

The first recorded words of man were a love song in the garden of sacred pleasure, a song of worship adoring God's most beautiful creation. Isn't that so cool. When the first man saw the first woman, he burst into worship. It doesn't appear very poetic in our English Bibles, yet it is a beautiful song in the Hebrew, just like the *Song of Songs*. When Adam saw Eve, he was no longer tempted to gawk at the glistening galaxies, mighty mountains, or sparkling rivers. His eyes were glued to God's most gorgeous achievement. Yet, as I said, we do not know what Eve looked like. Maybe she would be dumpy and ugly in our estimation. Knowing God the way I do, that is entirely possible. But whatever she looked like, her soon-to-be husband was blown away by her beauty. Solomon believed his wife was a work of art crafted by the master Artist of the universe (Song of Songs 7:1).

Every husband should believe that. Isn't that what King Jesus our Bridegroom believes? His blood is the sacrificial paint that restores the stunning beauty of his bride.

This was far from a comprehensive study on how to be a godly husband. I think it's just a bit of a primer. Every husband who calls himself a Christian ought to do his absolute best to imitate the two great husbands of Scripture. A selfless, sacrificial, gracious, and adoring husband is the picture that is crafted in the word of God. This kind of man will be a place of safety and an oasis of refreshment. *His love will be better than wine.* Wholeheartedly strive to be that husband for the soul that you have been charged to protect.

CHAPTER 6

Wives

How sobering it is to realize that our behavior has the potential to discredit the gospel. But how exciting it is to think that we can actually commend the gospel!

As verse 10 says, we can "adorn" the gospel with our lives. To "adorn" means to put something beautiful or attractive on display—like placing a flawless gemstone in a setting that uniquely shows off its brilliance. The gospel is like the most valuable of jewels. It is the pearl of great price.

Make no mistake, by adorning the gospel, we are not enhancing or improving it. The gospel cannot be improved! But by cultivating the feminine qualities listed in Titus 2, we can present the gospel as attractive, impressive, and pleasing to the watching world....

Consider the loveliness of a woman who passionately adores her husband, who tenderly cherishes her children, who creates a warm and peaceful home, who exemplifies purity, self-control, and kindness in her character and who gladly submits to her husband's leadership—for all the days God grants her life. I dare say there are few things that display the gospel jewel with greater elegance.[9]

But as for you, teach what accords with sound doctrine. Older men are to be sober-minded, dignified, self-controlled, sound in faith, in love, and in steadfastness. Older women likewise are to be reverent in behavior, not slanderers or slaves to much wine. They are to teach what is good, and so train the young women to love their husbands and children, to be self-controlled, pure, working at home, kind, and submissive to their own husbands, that the word of God may not be reviled. Likewise, urge the younger men to be self-controlled. Show yourself in all respects

> to be a model of good works, and in your teaching show integrity, dignity, and sound speech that cannot be condemned, so that an opponent may be put to shame, having nothing evil to say about us. Bondservants are to be submissive to their own masters in everything; they are to be well-pleasing, not argumentative, not pilfering, but showing all good faith, so that in everything they may adorn the doctrine of God our Savior. (Titus 2:1–10 ESV)

Wives were created by God to strengthen their husbands. Two primary ways husbands can be encouraged is through profuse admiration and passionate affection. Certainly, women are called to love others, especially their children. However, the Bible teaches that the best thing a mother can do for her children is to love their daddy first. I think it is rare for a Christian mother to be neglectful of her children. However, it's not so rare for a Christian wife to serve her husband leftovers. And I am not talking about food. This is especially true once children are born into the household. All the mothers I know never do this deliberately. The introduction of a child into the family is overwhelming and exhausting, especially for our wives. But without the training and guidance of biblically taught older women, it is pretty much impossible for this neglect not to occur. A new, tiny infant is helpless in every way, so baby receives Mom's constant attention. Daddy is anything but helpless, so he is unintentionally left to himself. On the island of Crete, Titus was given the responsibility to make sure the older women were trained in the wisdom of the Word. Only then would they be given the ministry of training the younger women. In my opinion, the greatest focus of the women's teaching ministry should be training the younger women to be godly wives and mothers. Titus chapter two is about how to build a healthy church by building healthy families. A church built on the wisdom of the Bible will make the gospel supremely attractive. Through the power of the Spirit and the wisdom of the Word, a woman can continue to be a strength to her man even with a home full of children. Of course, the only way this will work is if the selfless leader of the family is fully engaged in serving his wife and children. Intimacy between husband and wife on every level can be strengthened if both are striving to be selfless servants. If a woman is married to a self-focused man, she will need much encouragement from her best friends to continue to trust God (1 Peter 3:1–6). My heart burns compassionately for the women I know who are in that situation.

After becoming empty nesters, my wife and I ended up being emergency foster parents to two troubled children. The experience sapped us of our diminishing energy every single day. I say diminishing because we were both nearing sixty years old. And yes, our bedroom love was a little less consistent, but our intimacy grew immensely in the year and a half that Ahleauna and Dante lived with us. I believe that's true because we both slipped it into high gear in serving one another and these two very needy children. When we did make love, it was more special because together in every way we worked as one every day. It truly was one of life's greatest experiences for Kelli and me. After the kids lived with us for about six months, I remember feeling unsettled and commenting to my wife, "Honey, I feel bad, because I feel like I'm a better dad to these kiddos than I was for my own children." Of course, that was true because I was on the other side of much Bible study and experience. It was then that I realized that we have to work much harder at helping our young marrieds know what we now know. Isn't that what the above verse is calling the mature disciples in the church to be focused on? Healthy families will not only be more attractive, but they will also be more evangelistic. This is certainly why Paul gives Titus the advice that he does.

Through the crazy challenges of life, how does a Christian woman continue to profusely admire and be passionately affectionate toward her husband? How does a wife fulfill her first God-given role? Remember from our earlier study that the woman was created to be a place of strength for her man. But how can an overwhelmed wife and mother do that when she is depleted of all her energy? Hopefully I can answer that question throughout this chapter. Before we progress any further, let's talk about the first challenge in Titus 2 for wives.

> These older women must train the younger women to love
> their husbands and their children. (Titus 2:4 NLT)

It is interesting to me that the word used for love in the above passage is not the Greek word *agape*. *Agape* is the Greek word for unconditional, selfless love. It describes the kind of love that says, "It doesn't matter how you treat me, I will always love you." It is the word used in Ephesians 5 for husbands. Actually, wives are never challenged in the New Testament to *agape* their husbands. The Greek word in the above verse is *phileo*. This word refers to tender affection. It seems women are naturally better at *agape* than men. So men are challenged where they are weaker. In marriage, wives tend to struggle more in the area of affection. So the Bible challenges women according to their weakness. I have known women who excel at unconditional love for their deadbeat husbands. They continue to make their dinners, wash their clothes, and serve them in many ways even though their man is an unvarnished jerk. But the affectionate feelings are long gone. This is the specific gender challenge for wives. It never ceases to amaze me how incredible the word of God is. The Maker of everything knows exactly what we need to be a great spouse. The challenge for husbands is to learn to be selfless with another sinner. Likewise, the challenge for wives is to learn to be affectionate toward the sinner they are married to. Can a Christian learn to love and admire someone who disappoints often? We are expected to love even our enemies, so yes, absolutely. The best time to be at your best is when your spouse is at their worst. Not easy stuff! Listen to this vulnerable quote from a sincere wife and mother:

I was afraid of failing at affection because it is so unnatural to me...so uncomfortable and awkward. I was convinced that the smallest effort would come off as strange, even repulsive, to my husband. Even though I took action, my head was still in a very negative place. Do you fear failing? Do you fear being bad at loving your husband, kids, and friends? You're not alone. It's why we don't try. We're scared of either being rejected or looking stupid or simply doing affection badly.[10]

My wife has no problem being affectionate toward our children and grandchildren. It's very natural for her to love them in this way. However, she has had to work at being affectionate toward me. I deeply appreciate all her efforts in this area. Even what she thinks are "little things" are huge to me. Both genders have some difficult and unnatural work to do in being a godly spouse. Men must learn *agape*. Likewise, women must learn *phileo*—tender and passionate affection.

Anyone who thinks they can be a godly spouse without plenty of prayer, guidance, and biblical knowledge is completely deluded. Being a great husband or wife is far beyond human wisdom, strength, and determination. Wives must begin with the right picture, the proper knowledge about their husbands. If you want to improve your health by eating a good diet, it is important that you have the right information. If you were taught that potato chips, gummy bears, and chocolate bars are the healthiest foods to eat, then no matter how sincere you are about your health, you are going to fail. This is absolutely true when it comes to something as difficult as marriage. It is vital that you have the proper information to create a healthy relationship with your husband. As the last chapter challenged your husbands, sisters, this chapter will be most challenging for you. So be prepared. I prayed mightily before I wrote it. My goal is not to crush or discourage but rather inspire.

> You have captured my heart,
> my treasure, my bride.

> You hold it hostage with one glance of your eyes,
>> with a single jewel of your necklace.
> Your love delights me,
>> my treasure, my bride.
> Your love is better than wine,
>> your perfume more fragrant than spices.
>> (Song of Songs 4:9–10 NLT)

Her love was "better than wine." Her affection was intoxicating. So why was that? My dear sisters, what we're going to look at is God's portrait of an ideal wife. The Holy Spirit chose this ancient wife to be the go-to picture for all wives. She is the older sister who teaches the younger women how to be continuously affectionate toward their husbands. I have found at least three reasons why the Shulammite's love was better than wine.

First and most important, she eagerly embraced God's wisdom concerning marriage. She joyfully accepted the only perfect information available on what it means to be a wife. Although I have no proof of this, I think it's possible that the Shulammite was also the Proverbs 31 woman. She could have been the hardworking homemaker and passionate lover pictured within the wisdom literature of the Bible. When she was young, she learned a relentless work ethic as a slave girl in Lebanon. In her youth, she was also taught about sexual intimacy by her mother.

> I would lead you
>> and bring you to my mother's house—
>> she who has taught me.
> I would give you spiced wine to drink,
>> the nectar of my pomegranates. (Song of Songs 8:2)

Here is a great Old Testament example of an older woman teaching a younger woman how to be a wife. Trained in hard work in the fields during the day and in intimacy at the supper table in the evening. And we know this table-training included sex because of the "spiced wine" metaphor. This would be a huge and difficult shift in how we train our children in the sensitive areas. I'm just reporting how our ancient brothers and sisters passed on God's wisdom to the next generation. I do think it would be a better way, if we could get there. Even if the Shulammite wasn't also the Proverbs 31 woman, it doesn't matter, because we are absolutely supposed to smash the wisdom of these books together to produce the right picture of a godly wife.

When it comes to affection, sexual intimacy is always either at or near the top of the list for your man. Since there is an immense amount of confusion surrounding his holy subject, let's look at why God created sex.

> *It's our responsibility to talk about it. It is our calling, as the body of believers, to share the good news of the gospel of Jesus Christ—and every version of the holy scriptures I've ever read talks openly and candidly about sex. It is a topic fiercely close to God's heart, a topic that flows from the pages of his word. A topic laced with affirmation, guidance, and reproof. God, after all, is the inventor of sex. We were made, by him, as sexual beings. So if it's a topic fiercely close to his heart, it must become a topic fiercely close to ours.[11]*

> *Sexual intimacy is a powerful picture of the gospel—of the degree of intimacy and ecstasy we are capable of having with God. The Christian marriage is designed to showcase this masterpiece.... Here's the takeaway: what you think about sex really matters. Having God's perspective on the topic, whether you are single or married, is a vital piece of your growth as a daughter of God.[12]*

FIVE REASONS GOD
CREATED SEXUAL INTIMACY

1. Procreation

It would be a mistake to believe that the only reason God

thought up the idea of sexual intimacy is for making babies. It may not even be the main reason. It is interesting that in the *Song of Songs*, a book that is loaded with sexual references, that procreation is not mentioned or even hinted at.

2. Pleasure

Unbridled pleasure is certainly a reason that God gave us the good gift of sex.

Drink water from your own cistern,
   running water from your own well.
Should your springs overflow in the streets,
   your streams of water in the public squares?
Let them be yours alone,
   never to be shared with strangers.
May your fountain be blessed,
   and may you rejoice in the wife of your youth.
A loving doe, a graceful deer—
   may her breasts satisfy you always,
   may you ever be intoxicated with her love.
Why, my son, be intoxicated with another man's wife?
   Why embrace the bosom of a wayward woman?
For your ways are in full view of the LORD,
   and he examines all your paths.
The evil deeds of the wicked ensnare them;
   the cords of their sins hold them fast.
For lack of discipline they will die,
led astray by their own great folly. (Proverbs 5:15–23)

In Proverbs five the father is teaching his son about the importance of faithfulness in marriage. Sometimes people are surprised to find this verse in the Bible. But God is not a prude or embarrassed of anything he ever created. I believe sex is one of his favorite gifts to us. God longs for us to get over our hang-ups and shame when it comes to this form of intimacy. Is that not one of the reasons we even have the *Song of Songs* in our Bibles? As a good father, I love it when my children enjoy the gifts that I give them. There is *nothing* dirty or worldly about sex if we handle this precious gift in the way God prescribed. If we do, sex is holy and is even an act of worship. God purposely engineered our bodies so that we could enjoy each other in marriage. He placed approximately 8000 highly sensitive nerve endings within a woman's "hidden place" (Song of Songs 7:2 Voice). Men have about half that many. (Hey, what's up with that?) What does it say about God that he would engineer our bodies like that? It says God *wants* us to enjoy extreme pleasure together. In the above passage, the wise father is teaching his son to enjoy his future wife's body. There is a double challenge in Proverbs 5. Husbands are challenged to be satisfied with their wives. And wives are called to be satisfying, even intoxicating.

A few years ago a couple came to me seeking advice on whether the wife should have a breast enhancement. With some indignation I asked, "You have the freedom to do whatever you want, but why aren't you satisfied with your wife? She's beautiful just the way God created her!" Your wife should be your standard of beauty, not what the world has fabricated.

It is very discouraging to live in a home atmosphere that does not have God's word as its standard because a husband is not following Christ. What can a godly wife do in such a situation? First, ponder, meditate, and pray through 1 Peter 2:18–3:6. 1 Peter is about how to live righteously through unfair suffering. Peter's advice is funneled through the cross of Christ. But even if you do not find peace with your temporary husband here on earth, you can find contentment with your eternal Spouse. Peter makes this point not only through Jesus but also through Sarah, the wife of Abraham. Sarah's deep trust in God is what made the difference when she couldn't trust her husband (Genesis12, 20). Study her, and in most situations you will know how to respond. Second, consider reading *How to Act Right When Your Spouse Acts Wrong* by Dr. Leslie Vernick. I highly recommend this book for those in difficult marriages. Third, deputize some of your best spiritual friends to pray and fast with you and to do this often. Ask them to help you overcome any discouragement and bitterness. Find sisters who will be empathetic but not sentimental.

3. Protection

Flee from sexual immorality. All other sins a person commits are outside the body, but whoever sins sexually, sins against their own body. Do you not know that your bodies are temples of the Holy Spirit, who is in you, whom you have received from God? You are not your own; you were bought at a price. Therefore honor God with your bodies.

Now for the matters you wrote about: "It is good for a man not to have sexual relations with a woman." But since sexual immorality is occurring, each man should have sexual relations with his own wife, and each woman with her own husband. The husband should fulfill his marital duty to his wife, and likewise the wife to her husband. The wife does not have authority over her own body but yields it to her husband. In the same way, the husband does not have authority over his own body but yields it to his wife. Do not deprive each other except perhaps by mutual consent and for a time, so that you may devote yourselves to prayer. Then come together again so that Satan will not tempt you because of your lack of self-control. I say this as a concession, not as a command. I wish that all of you were as I am. But each of you has your own gift from God; one has this gift, another has that. (1 Corinthians 6:18–7:7)

The Greeks taught that the body was bad, and this crooked thinking slipped into the church. The body isn't bad; it is very good, as God created it to be. Just because we've done many bad things with our bodies doesn't change their original value. The reason we wear clothing is not because our bodies are ugly, but quite the opposite; it's because they're beautiful. Whatever happened in Genesis 3 reworked our "insides" in such a way that we cannot handle seeing each other unclothed. In 1 Corinthians 6 Paul makes a bold statement emphasizing the importance of what we do with our bodies. Our souls *and* our bodies are a temple of the Holy Spirit, so it matters very much what we do with our bodies. When Jesus returns, the true value of our bodies will be realized through the fact that they too, along with our souls, will be resurrected.

The proper use of a single temple is to run away from sex. The proper use of a married temple is to enjoy sex. The two concepts became mixed, and this is the confused thinking that Paul is trying to unravel for the Corinthian church. To abstain from sexual intimacy for any reason other than something as important as prayer leaves your spouse vulnerable to temptation. Certainly if they cave in to that temptation, it is their fault. They should have exercised more self-control. However, you helped usher them into an arena of higher temptation because of your lack of love. This is why Paul gives the challenge to both husbands and wives to not deprive their spouse of intimate pleasure. In our hypersexualized world, it is vital that husbands and wives take care of each other. No, sexual intimacy is not more important than its cousin, emotional intimacy. But there is one big difference between these two forms of intimacy. If a wife is struggling emotionally and her husband is inept at helping her out, she has other outlets. She can go to her best friends and pour out her soul. However, if either wife or husband is struggling sexually, there is no other outlet. You can't share even a hint of sexual intimacy with anyone other than your spouse (Ephesians 5:3). My dear sisters, do not leave your husband "in Gethsemane" to struggle all by himself. The apostles fell asleep on Jesus, and he had to fight off the temptations of the flesh alone. To deprive your husband of sexual intimacy pretty much does the same thing. Like his Lord, he shouldn't fall, but please remember he is not Jesus. So whatever you do, do not put sex with your husband on the same to-do list as washing dishes, doing the laundry, or making yummy dinners. I think I speak for a good number of men when I say that I would rather eat peanut butter sandwiches and consistently enjoy sex with my wife than have her slaving for hours over fancy dinners. I am grateful when she makes those tasty meals, but if she can't do both, bedroom love is a much better way to strengthen my soul. Sometimes it is the husband who wrestles with the lower desire for sexual intimacy. For help with this, refer to *Intimate Issues* by Linda Dillow and Lorraine Pintus.

Sisters, remember why you were created. You were created to be a place of strength for the man that God brought into your life. Nothing strengthens your man like being deeply connected to the woman he adores.

4. Power

> The heavens declare the glory of God;
>> the skies proclaim the work of his hands.
> Day after day they pour forth speech;
>> night after night they reveal knowledge.
> They have no speech, they use no words;
>> no sound is heard from them.
> Yet their voice goes out into all the earth,
>> their words to the ends of the world.
> In the heavens God has pitched a tent for the sun.
>> It is like a bridegroom coming out of his chamber,
>> like a champion rejoicing to run his course.
> It rises at one end of the heavens
>> and makes its circuit to the other;
>> nothing is deprived of its warmth. (Psalm 19:1–6)

Healthy intimacy immensely strengthens marriage. The above passage teaches that God's creation displays his crafts- manship. The heavens reveal great truths about who God is.

When you look at the galaxies, you can be filled with strength because you can discover how broad his shoulders are. David specifically picks the sun and brags about how it points to God. In attempting to describe the sun, he uses a metaphor of sexual intimacy to boast about its power. Basically, he says that a brilliant sunrise reminds him of a husband who has just enjoyed sexual intimacy with his wife. As the radiant sun bursts above the horizon, a husband bursts out of his front door to meet the day. He is deeply connected with his covenant partner, so he is powerfully energized. Women, you were handcrafted by God to bring strength to your husband through your different thinking, emotions, and body. This is quite deep, and I encourage each married couple to ponder it. Like the sun, selfless bedroom love unveils great things about God. That leads us to our final point about why God created sexual intimacy.

5. Picture

Sex is a picture of the indescribable joy of God. Doesn't the immense pleasure that a husband and wife enjoy together while creating a child point to the joy that overwhelmed the Divine Family as they created us, even you? Absolutely! I believe God enjoyed every second as you were being created, wonderfully and uniquely handcrafted by Father, Son, and Spirit to be an image-bearing gift to everyone around you. God carefully knit you together for a special purpose. And when you strive to live according to his will, you bring him unspeakable joy. Even though our children have flaws and are very different, Kelli and I are mesmerized by the unique beauty each of them holds. God has the same deep fascination for every one of us. Do not let Satan cause you to believe otherwise. Another way that sex mimics the joy of God is that it briefly points to the never-ending joy that the three experience together. Sexual intimacy has revealed to me that God is much different from the frowning deity that many people believe in. He is not guilty of being a cosmic killjoy. If that were truly his character, he never would have come up with the idea of sexual intimacy in the first place. Furthermore, the potential of joy that we can find in bedroom love points to the joyous intimacy we can find with our spiritual Bridegroom. The more deeply I am connected with King Jesus, the more I am filled with an inexpressible joy. Married sexual intimacy also prophesies and points to the eternal joys of heaven.

Sex is a bit like an X-ray—a Symbolic Eschatological X-ray. An X-ray is a faint and foggy picture of something you can't see with the naked eye. It gives you some truths, but not the complete reality. It is accurate, but much is missing. Eschatology is the study of what happens when Jesus returns. If we embrace sexual intimacy as God designed it, it can be like a fuzzy X-ray that reveals some incomplete yet amazing truths about our future with God. As I wrote about earlier, this is why Satan despises sex. He does not want you to get a hint of the eternal joys that await us. If you do, you will shout the good news of the gospel from the rooftops. So each and every day Satan is striving to ruin the intimacy between you and your spouse. I have listed five good reasons why wives should make sure that sexual intimacy is a priority in their relationship with their husband. As King Solomon became an emotional expert for his wife, his wife became a "sex-pert" for her king. They both became strong in the area that the other needed most. I have often wondered why what wives need from their husbands is the area we tend to be weakest in. I think you can flip that around—it's generally true for wives also. Possibly, it's because the challenge to be what you naturally are not will cause you to desperately rely on Jesus. We are always better if we feel so weak that we cannot do what we're called to do without the Lord. Somehow, at least for a little while, Solomon and his wife became what they needed to be for each other. I believe their marriage is the most imitable because their story was handpicked by God the Holy Spirit to be in the Bible.

The Proverbs 31 woman is the builder of many rooms in

the home, and her theological running mate, the Shulammite, is the builder of the bedroom. Let's remember that the *Song of Songs* is a book about healthy intimacy in all its forms, not just sexual intimacy. Understanding this helps some to not resist its message. The very fact that we have an entire book in the Bible about intimacy underscores the importance of this area in our lives. To expend yourself in serving others while letting your intimacy with your spouse go by the wayside is not the picture of a prophetic marriage. The wise homebuilder of the *Song of Songs* has much to teach us about covenant intimacy.

THE SHULAMMITE

The Shulammite understood the "why's" of sexual intimacy. She was an eager learner from both her mother and her husband, Solomon. An entire book could be written on this subject, so this will not be comprehensive, but I will focus on two specific ideas. In her relationship with her husband, the Shulammite strengthened the soul of her husband through persistent admiration and passionate affection.

Persistent Admiration (Respect)

In the beginning stages of falling in love, it is common to express profuse adoration for one another. Anytime you are around a bride-to-be she cannot stop talking about how awesome her man is. Persisting in that positive mindset is what the wife in the Song does so very well. After they are wedded and she sees his hidden flaws, she learns to give him undeserved admiration. The only bachelor that a woman could ever marry that she wouldn't have to often fight against her own flesh to respect is Jesus himself. Since he's not available until the end of this present age, every bride-to-be should be well prepared for this struggle. Let's take a peek at *Song of Songs* chapter five.

She

I slept but my heart was awake.
  Listen! My beloved is knocking:
"Open to me, my sister, my darling,
  my dove, my flawless one.
My head is drenched with dew,
  my hair with the dampness of the night."
I have taken off my robe—
  must I put it on again?
I have washed my feet—
  must I soil them again?
My beloved thrust his hand through the latch-opening;
  my heart began to pound for him.
I arose to open for my beloved,
  and my hands dripped with myrrh,
my fingers with flowing myrrh,
  on the handles of the bolt.
I opened for my beloved,
  but my beloved had left; he was gone.
  My heart sank at his departure.
I looked for him but did not find him.
  I called him but he did not answer.
The watchmen found me
  as they made their rounds in the city.
They beat me, they bruised me;
  they took away my cloak,
  those watchmen of the walls!
Daughters of Jerusalem, I charge you—
  if you find my beloved,
what will you tell him?
  Tell him I am faint with love.

Friends

How is your beloved better than others,
  most beautiful of women?

How is your beloved better than others,
that you so charge us?

She
My beloved is radiant and ruddy,
outstanding among ten thousand.
His head is purest gold;
his hair is wavy
and black as a raven.
His eyes are like doves
by the water streams,
washed in milk,
mounted like jewels.
His cheeks are like beds of spice
yielding perfume.
His lips are like lilies
dripping with myrrh.
His arms are rods of gold
set with topaz.
His body is like polished ivory
decorated with lapis lazuli.
His legs are pillars of marble
set on bases of pure gold.
His appearance is like Lebanon,
choice as its cedars.
His mouth is sweetness itself;
he is altogether lovely.
This is my beloved, this is my friend,
daughters of Jerusalem. (Song of Songs 5:2–16)

This section of the poetry appears to be a scene from later in their marriage. It appears that Solomon comes home extremely late at night, because the dew is already upon the foliage. Since he is the busy king of an entire country, his arriving late is probably a common occurrence in their marriage. Despite the lateness of the hour, Solomon initiates sex with his half-asleep wife. He gently sweet-talks her in the hope of enjoying some spicy love. However, she is not having it. In this intimate scene, who is being selfish? Some theologians say that he is, and others accuse her of selfishness. I think the poetry is so flexible that it could be either or both, depending on the circumstances. Maybe they just spent some time the night before, and he is the guilty party. Or maybe it's been a while, and she should rise to the occasion. Two selfless people can figure out the solution in such situations. Husbands and wives need to be highly allergic to selfishness, the intimacy killer. Let's march through this Holy Spirit–authored passage verse by verse.

Song of Songs 5:2–3

An exhausted Solomon comes home from a long day at work in the hope of ending that day in the arms of his lover. It's crazy how differently I am wired than the woman that I am married to. When I am depleted from the day, one of the first things on my mind is being connected with Kelli in our bedroom. This is also true when I am feeling troubled or discouraged about something. Guess what, she is wired completely the opposite of that. Who wired up our inner beings? Why did God make us so opposite in so many ways? It's almost like he is "forcing" selflessness! It's like he is pushing us to figure it out and become servant lovers of one another.

The Shulammite is also weary from the day and is drifting off to sleep. The floors of ancient castles were not all that clean, so she doesn't want to go to the trouble of having to wash her feet again. Don't believe the Hollywood versions of intimacy. They always make it so easy and trouble-free. But any of us who have been married for any length of time know that real life is not like that. Connecting emotionally or sexually is often fraught with misunderstandings, awkwardness, insecurities, and an inner resistance. These negative feelings can spoil the mood very quickly. Which is exactly what happens to our couple. Remember that this one scene from their marriage may represent a season in their life together. All married people go through seasons like this that sometimes even last for years. That is where the phrase comes from, "I guess the honeymoon is over."

Song of Songs 5:4

Solomon is not so easily dissuaded, so he continues to try to awaken her desires.

Song of Songs 5:5–6

After some time he finally gives up. However, his persistent advances have awakened her passion. But it is too late. He is either asleep by her side or has exited to his own royal suite. In those days, kings usually had their own bedroom. So now it appears the tables are turned and she is ready to go, but he is gone.

Song of Songs 5:7

Her awakened desire to connect with her husband is described metaphorically in her searching the city. This didn't actually happen, because that would have been very inappropriate for a queen. In her search she runs into the watchmen of the city. They are symbolic stand-ins for her conscience, which is now giving her a beatdown. She is feeling guilty that she did not take care of her husband. She was created to strengthen him, and now she's feeling like she dropped the ball. Sometimes guilt like this is appropriate, and sometimes it's not. It is vital that we have a well-trained, biblically informed conscience. Some people struggle with unnecessary guilt, and others disregard their conscience. The healthy way to respond to an appropriately troubled conscience is to graciously forget what is behind and then go after what your conscience is prompting you to do. This is described in the rest of chapter 5.

Song of Songs 5:8–9

It appears that the next day she gets together with her

best friends and pours out her troubled soul. In the days be-fore phones and text messaging, there was pretty much no way to get in touch with someone, unless of course you sent out a human messenger. She charges her friends that if they see her husband they let him know she is "faint with love." She is feeling insecure and is wondering what he is thinking. When we are being accosted by our consciences, we are especially vulnerable to giving in to the flesh. You have to read between the lines of the poetry, but it certainly appears that she is saying some nega-tive things about her husband to her friends. She may have said something like, "I can't believe how selfish he was last night. It was after midnight and he wanted to..." This "lucky" lady had chosen some good spiritual friends, because they don't let her immerse herself in negativity toward her man. They are empa-thetic but not sentimental. They are not going to let her continue to bash her imperfect but amazing husband, so they skillfully guide her to remember all his great characteristics. It's like they are saying, "Just a few days ago you were bragging about how awesome he is, and now you're complaining that he is a selfish clod!" She responds to their gentle yet pointed discipling and ponders deeply on his great qualities, a "Titus 2 ministry" a thousand years before Paul even wrote about it.

Song of Songs 5:10–16

She remembers that he is "outstanding among ten thousand." Which is a way of saying "He's a keeper," or "I married the most eligible bachelor on the planet." His eyes are doves. So even though his actions are not always perfect, she realizes that he has a good soul. His "arms are rods of gold." This doesn't necessarily mean he looks like a bodybuilder. She is appreciating his great strength and character. He is a man's man in the best sense of the word. Furthermore, it indicates in verse 15 that he is a pillar in the community because of his good character. His mouth is "sweetness itself" because he is so encouraging and therefore his kisses are intoxicating (Song of Songs 7:9). After she takes the time to meditate on his godly qualities, she realizes that he is her very best friend. Remembering your husband's strong characteristics is much easier if you consistently express them. The biblical practice of praising your spouse is a proactive way of keeping you from developing a negative mindset.

Since Genesis chapter 3 it has been too easy to become negative toward one another. It takes great intentionality to persist in admiration, especially in marriage. This humble queen has deputized her friends to not let her become a dripping-faucet wife (Proverbs 19:13, 27:15). As frustration, criticism, and nagging do not create a radiant wife, neither does negativity strengthen the soul of a husband. One of the greatest ways to end up with the kind of husband you desire is to persevere in giving him undeserved encouragement. The next time we see them together, she is giving him the love that he was asking for in their late-night encounter (Song of Songs 6:1–3). The results are a happy husband and a wife with a peaceful conscience. Furthermore, the oneness between them has been deepened rather than diminished (6:3).

Admiration must be expressed for it to do its good work. One of the chief ways that this godly woman convinced her husband that she respected him was through her eyes. The greatest way to communicate what is in your heart is through the "windows of your soul." The adoring and unbroken gaze from the soul of a wife is one of the most powerful forces on earth. That is not an exaggeration! I have a scripture to prove it:

> Turn your eyes from me;
>> they overwhelm me.
> Your hair is like a flock of goats
>> descending from Gilead. (Song of Songs 6:5)

Thousands of people go to eye-gazing seminars to find meaningful connection with another human being. The above verse reveals that eye-gazing is one of the most powerful ways to communicate admiration to your spouse. Sometimes my wife thinks I'm crazy, because I tell her that she can "slay me with her eyes." But I am not crazy, because that is exactly what the poetry is saying in the above verse. What is truly amazing is that King Solomon, one of the most powerful men on the planet, is being overwhelmed by the adoring stare of an ex–slave girl, the "ugly duckling" of Lebanon. Joyful, approving looks—or the opposite: angry glances—have a huge impact on a husband's heart. They build up or tear down. Solomon asks his wife to turn away because he cannot stand the flood of encouragement that is exiting her soul into his. The admiration that she felt in her heart poured out through her eyes. It's a fact: your eyes often communicate much more truth than your words. The Shulammite learned the most effective way to relay what she felt so deeply in her soul.

> Your neck is like an ivory tower.
> Your eyes are the pools of Heshbon
>   by the gate of Bath Rabbim.
> Your nose is like the tower of Lebanon
>   looking toward Damascus. (Song of Songs 7:4)

The pools of Heshbon were deep, manufactured reservoirs of abundant refreshing water. Heshbon was a lush and fertile area on the east side of the Red Sea, which is surrounded by desert. The cool water from these pools refreshed weary desert travelers. Like these pools, the Shulammite was also "man-made." Or better said, she was remade by her king's love. Overwhelming gratitude poured out from the deep reservoir of her soul. She was thankful for his love, and she communicated that clearly and often through her eyes.

Whatever you truly feel about your man is relayed to him by how you do or don't look at him. Dear Sisters, use your eyes to captivate your husband, because someone else might be trying to.

Don't lust for her beauty.

Don't let her coy glances seduce you. (Proverbs 6:25 NLT)

When I look into your eyes,... there's so much they hold. —Jason Mraz & Michael Natter

One of the main reasons why the Shulammite's love was intoxicating is because she persisted in admiration. She remained convinced, so what was within her heart spilled out upon her husband.

Passionate Affection

It appears that her growing admiration was a catalyst for her passionate affection. In the beginning of their relationship, the reason she was so eager for intimacy was because of her adoration of him (Song of Songs 1:1–4). As a man should not let his love die through the challenges of marriage, so a wife should not let her respect diminish. Each has a challenge to overcome by the power of the Holy Spirit. It stands to reason that if she deeply admires him she will passionately desire him. Furthermore, if a man isn't consistently desired by his wife, it will be difficult to convince him that she admires him. This tentative woman learned to be an initiator and an instigator in the bedroom. Here is a well-informed quote that helps give proper meaning to this passionate poetry:

> *The lovers discover in themselves an Eden, thriving and abundant, a Promised Land of vines and fig trees, pomegranates, wheat, milk and honey. The poet's metaphors keep shifting between the actual landscape, suffused with erotic associations, and the landscape of the body. The Shulammite waits for her lover in a garden, but she herself is a garden; the two of them go out to the fragrant vineyards to make love, but she herself is a vineyard, her breasts like clusters of grapes, and their kisses an intoxicating wine.*[13]

What the poetry is saying, especially in *Song of Songs* chapter seven, is that she is a garden of holy pleasure for her husband, although not for his selfish pleasure. If in reading this book thus far you are still tempted to think that God is a prude concerning sexual pleasure, then *Song of Songs* chapter seven should put the nail in the coffin of your concept of a "cosmic killjoy God."

> Him: Your feet are so beautiful,
>> *perfectly fitted* in sandals, noble daughter!
>
> Your sculpted thighs are like jewels,
>> the work of a master hand.
>
> Your hidden place is *open to me* like a goblet, *perfect and round,*
>> that never runs dry of blended wine;
>
> Your waist is a mound of wheat—*curved and white and fertile*—
>> encircled by lilies.
>
> Your breasts are like two fawns,
>> twins of a gazelle.
>
> Your neck is as *stunning* as an ivory tower;
>> your eyes *shimmer* like the pools in Heshbon
>> by the gate of Bath-rabbim.
>
> Your nose is *strong and proud* like the tower of Lebanon,
>> which points toward Damascus.
>
> Your head is as stately as Mount Carmel;
>> your hair *shines* like a tapestry of royal purple cloth—
>> the king is held captive by your locks.
>
> How beautiful you are, my love, and how pleasing
>> In all your delightful *and satisfying* ways.
>
> Your stature is as elegant as a date palm tree,
>> and your breasts are sweet, *attractive, and round* like clusters of its fruit.
>
> I say, "I will climb the palm tree;
>> I will take hold of its fruit."
>
> May your breasts be like clusters of grapes,

> the fragrance of your mouth like *fresh* apples,
> and may your kisses *satisfy* like the best wine.
>
> Her: *May the wine* go down smoothly for my love,
>   flowing gently over his lips and teeth.
> I belong to my love,
>   and he has desire for me. (Song of Songs 7:1–10 Voice)

Let me say a few things before we look at this passage. For many women, this is the most uncomfortable chapter in the Bible. It is unmistakable what is happening. This grinning husband is mesmerized by his unclothed wife. From head to toe, he admires every part of her. We must remember that this chapter is written by God the Holy Spirit, not some oversexed guy who found a way to slip it into the canon of Scripture. Sisters, the reason your husband loves to see you naked is because God made him that way. There is everything good, right, and even holy about that.

Many years ago a sex worker was being interviewed on a talk show. She was questioned as to why so many married men seek after women like her. I don't recall what talk show it was or anyone's name, including hers. I only remember what she said. She looked at the women in the audience and said, "Your husbands don't come to me because I look the way I do, but because they desire passion. Stop worrying about how you look and give your husbands some passion." I kid you not, that is what she said. Of course, it is never ever OK for a man to be unfaithful even if he is married to a wife who is "locked up" (Song of Songs 4:12). The only right response is to love her as Jesus loves.

After the wear and tear of having some children and gaining a few pounds, wives often believe that they don't have what it takes anymore to be exciting in the bedroom. Let me say something very important: you are absolutely the *only* one who has what it takes for your husband. If a man goes somewhere else, it will completely ruin his life, even his eternity. You are his lifelong covenant partner. He has entrusted his entire sexual life to you and to you only. Personally, I have never been more attracted to everything about my wife, including her body, which is on the precipice of being sixty years old. What she sees as flaws, I see as beautiful. Learn to be unashamed and confident, and regardless of your body type, your husband will be completely crazy about you. If he's not, there is something desperately wrong with him, and hopefully he will get some help. It's a good practice for husbands and wives to keep themselves in reasonable shape. However, regardless of how hard you fight against the aging process, your body sooner or later is going to become at least a little droopy. I work out now, mostly for health and vibrancy. At sixty-two, my body is getting a little droopy no matter what I do. As a younger husband, I used to nag my wife about working out. That always backfired with her, because every time I said something, what she heard was that I was disappointed by how she looked. Now that I have repented of my worldliness, she is inspired to take care of herself. Nagging never works for either gender.

If, when getting close in the bedroom, you are preoccupied with body anxiety, then do the hard work and train your brain to be fully engaged in the moment. Be preoccupied with loving and serving your husband. The Bible does say not to worry about anything (Philippians 4). If you are married to a man who has complained about your looks, your husband definitely needs some good counsel. The Bible says that "beauty is fleeting" (Proverbs 31:30). Therefore we should emphasize the deeper, lasting things rather than mere physical attractiveness, which is all too often governed far too much by the standards of the world. Complaining never helps a woman confidently live within the skin that God put her in. There are far better ways to inspire a woman. Husbands, if you want your wife to become uninhibited, then you're going to have to believe she is the most beautiful person on earth. You be convinced of that and then you will be able to convince her of it.

If you believe that God is down on you, you are going to look down on others, especially your spouse. Your "critical god" is going to cause you to be critical of others. I believe that God thinks I'm amazing. I am confident that he not only loves me, but he also likes me. I'm worth so much to him that he was willing to die for me. I'm sure that sounds really arrogant. I believe that, not because I'm so awesome, but rather because God is. I am acutely aware of my shortcomings and flaws, but for the most part, my weaknesses don't determine how I see myself anymore. I finally really do believe God looks past those things because of the blood of Christ. Unless you are living a lifestyle dominated by deliberate sinning, you should believe that God adores you. That mindset reveals a healthy relationship with your spiritual Bridegroom. I think all three of my children are totally awesome. Even as I write this, I'm holding back from bragging about each one of them. I see their flaws very clearly. Along with my wife I raised them, so I know them. But I am blown away at how incredible they are. Our Father in heaven is the same way. When you believe your Father (or husband) is proud of you, you are motivated to live in such a way that makes him proud. People who believe they are beautiful, act beautiful. If they are led well, eventually Christians should not be plagued with chronic negative self-esteem issues. Well-nourished souls become healthy and secure in their relationship with God (1 Timothy 4:6–8).

The *Song of Songs* is allotted the double task of pointing to both temporary and eternal marriages. Solomon's adoration of the Shulammite portrays how King Jesus views us. This is the deeper meaning of Song of Songs seven.

The metaphors of chapter seven give rich instructions revealing how a loving husband views sexual intimacy. The wife should not recoil at her husband's fascination with her body, but should rather be encouraged by it. Her breasts are mentioned three different times in the chapter. So if her husband loves to focus on that part (or any part) of her body, she shouldn't be put off. God made her beautiful, so she should relax, cherish her husband's love, and enjoy the moment. I chose The Voice translation for this Scripture reference because it is the only version that is unashamed enough to render verse 2 accurately. She may have a beautiful belly button (NIV, ESV, CSB, NLT, KJV), but that is not what he is enthralled with. He is attracted to and intoxicated by her "hidden place" (vulva). Her body is likened to a chalice of wine that he can sip from often because it never runs dry. The poetry teaches that he is attracted to every part of her.

> I belong to my beloved,
>> and his desire is for me. (Song of Songs 7:10)

If she was plagued with the temptation to think that all he cares about is her body, she is no longer. She is convinced that he desires *her.*

Why does a man desire bedroom love so much and so often? For the same reason that a good mother aches to be close to her children. They are always on her mind because they came from her body. She longs to be close to what used to be inside her. Likewise, a man desires to be intimately one with what God took out of him (Genesis 2:21–22). The consistent desire a man has for his wife is just as legitimate as that of a woman for her children. A husband feels closest to his wife in the bedroom because that's when they are closest. What is more intimate than a man being inside his wife? It would be a terrible thing if a selfish man cut his wife off from seeing their children. Likewise, a man who is consistently stiff-armed in the bedroom suffers much loneliness.

> *(to him)* Come out into the fields, my love,
>> and there spend the night in the villages.
> Let's rise with the morning and go to the vineyards
>> to see if the vines have budded,
> If their blossoms have opened,
>> and if the pomegranates are in bloom.

> There I will give you my love.
> The mandrakes send out their seductive fragrance,
>   and the finest fruits wait at our doors—
> New pleasures as well as old—
>   I have stored them up for you, my lover.
>   (Song of Songs 7:11–13 Voice)

The wife of this very blessed husband learned to go far beyond bedroom compliance. As he was passionate for her, she became passionate for him. A noticeable theme in the Song is that this couple never seems to be able to get enough alone time together. This is a common struggle for most married couples, especially with the arrival of children. Instead of growing discouraged or resentful about this challenge, the Shulammite plans a romantic getaway. She gives her busy king a steamy invitation, which I am guessing he gratefully accepted. She flirtatiously lets him know that she has stored up for him "new pleasures as well as old." She now has a whole new set of "luggage" to bring on their trip. With the help of God, her gracious husband, and her friends, she has thrown out the old negative baggage. Her new bags are full of husband-pleasing intimate love, and her selfless spirit blesses both of them. She now enjoys the bedroom every bit as much as he does.

Creativity is an important key to building healthy emotional and sexual intimacy. Wives are often hurt by their husband's lack of engagement in conversation. Shallow dialogue punctuated with one-word answers does not facilitate emotional oneness. Engaging in a conversation while wanting to be somewhere else isn't any better. My wife always knows, and so does yours, if I would rather not be in a conversation with her. We can also flip this around. A husband always knows if his wife would rather not be in a "sexual conversation." Sex is a powerful form of communication between husband and wife. What do we as a husband or a wife consistently communicate to our spouse? *"Let's get this conversation over with so I can get back to the game, or go to sleep,"* hurts much more than it helps. Checking the scores or anxiously thinking about tomorrow's schedule when you should be totally focused on your spouse is very discouraging. Both genders do this to each other, so no one should be wagging a self-righteous finger. Instead, we should realize our selfish tendencies and strive to overcome them, so we can become a servant lover to the person we vowed to love wholeheartedly. Be committed to overcoming, because on the other side of perseverance and self-denial are extraordinarily rich intimate blessings.

I will not specifically get into what "old and new" sexual pleasures might be. There are many good books that you can refer to for creative ideas. Two selfless people can figure these things out with little drama. I recommend *The Art of Intimate Marriage* by Tim and Dr. Jennifer Konzen.

It seems the most common reasons given for putting off your hopeful husband are weariness and headaches. Sometimes these are the results of or camouflage for other, deeper issues that must be attended to. However, it is well documented that if you have more sex you will have fewer headaches and more energy. Marital sex is one of the healthiest things that you can engage in. During soul-bonding sex, your body and brain are bathed in chemicals that reduce hypertension and promote better sleep. Well-connected spouses are happier and have stronger immune systems. They actually live longer. The reasons that women often use to put off sex until later can be proactively lessened by engaging in the very thing they do not want to do at the moment. "But I don't have time!" People make time for what is most important to them. From our study, bedroom love should be a high priority. Certainly, there are seasons in our lives when we are pressed for time. Raising children can wreak havoc on your already overly busy life. The bedroom can become a place of nearly no sex, or at best, sleepy-eyed quickies. But even exhausted quickies can be an incredible experience between lovers if in that brief moment you are fully engaged. Dutiful quickies usually backfire into frustration and guilt. With most couples, spontaneity is more desirable, but in the busiest times of life, scheduling special time is a must, or it usually doesn't happen.

My final comment about all this is that being fully engaged and creative emotionally or sexually convinces your spouse that you deeply care for them, and that their heartfelt needs are also felt deeply within your heart.

I will end this discussion about sex with some sage advice from Sam Laing:

It is time for married couples to claim their gifts. It is time for husbands and wives to shed the unbiblical shackles of a mechanistic, boring and routine sex life. It is time to cast aside false modesty and the false belief that sex, and the environment of our spouse's body and their enjoyment of ours, is somehow tainted, twisted or perverted.[14]

A wise woman builds her home,
  but a foolish woman tears it down with her own hands.
    (Proverbs 14:1 NLT)

A house is built by wisdom
  and becomes strong through good sense.
Through knowledge its rooms are filled
  with all sorts of precious riches and valuables.
    (Proverbs 24:3–4 NLT)

THE PROVERBS 31 WOMAN

Wives are called to be homebuilders (Titus 2:3–5). They are uniquely created by God to strengthen their husbands and nurture their children. As she embraces the wisdom of the Bible, a God-wise woman will fill each room of the home with beautiful treasures. The Proverbs 31 woman is surrendered within the bigger part of her home, and the Holy Spirit can work mightily through her surrender. The *Song of Songs* is a portrait of a wife surrendered to God in the bedroom. Paint these two images on

the same canvas and you have what God says is a heroic wife.
Let's take a brief look at Proverbs 31.

> A wife of noble character who can find?
>   She is worth far more than rubies.
> Her husband has full confidence in her
>   and lacks nothing of value.
> She brings him good, not harm,
>   all the days of her life.
> She selects wool and flax
>   and works with eager hands.
> She is like the merchant ships,
>   bringing her food from afar.
> She gets up while it is still night;
>   she provides food for her family
>   and portions for her female servants.
> She considers a field and buys it;
>   out of her earnings she plants a vineyard.
> She sets about her work vigorously;
>   her arms are strong for her tasks.
> She sees that her trading is profitable,
>   and her lamp does not go out at night.
> In her hand she holds the distaff
>   and grasps the spindle with her fingers.
> She opens her arms to the poor
>   and extends her hands to the needy.
> When it snows, she has no fear for her household;
>   for all of them are clothed in scarlet.
> She makes coverings for her bed;
>   she is clothed in fine linen and purple.
> Her husband is respected at the city gate,
>   where he takes his seat among the elders of the land.
> She makes linen garments and sells them,
>   and supplies the merchants with sashes.
> She is clothed with strength and dignity;

she can laugh at the days to come.
She speaks with wisdom,
and faithful instruction is on her tongue.
She watches over the affairs of her household
and does not eat the bread of idleness.
Her children arise and call her blessed;
her husband also, and he praises her:
"Many women do noble things,
but you surpass them all."
Charm is deceptive, and beauty is fleeting;
but a woman who fears the LORD is to be praised.
Honor her for all that her hands have done,
and let her works bring her praise at the city gate.
(Proverbs 31:10–31)

Life is primarily about relationships. Therefore the wisdom literature centers on how to be successful relationally. So let's organize our thoughts about Proverbs 31 in that way.

When it comes to relationships, the Proverbs 31 woman is an expert. She has learned to love many without leaving those she is supposed to primarily love wanting in the wake of an overly busy lifestyle. If you step back from this all-important passage you discover that she has a life outside the home. She has a job (Song of Songs 31:16) and extends her hands to the needy (Song of Songs 31:20). However, the emphasis in this instructive poetry is that her husband and home are her top priority and get the most of her energy. Most likely, as in New Testament times, her way of extending her love to the poor was through hospitality, so her evangelism and outreach didn't take her constantly out of the home. Her peaceful and happy home was her greatest advertisement for God. I say this because I have often seen women cringe when they read this wisdom-packed passage. It overwhelms them just to read it. However, within this passage are truths that will help you not to spread yourself too thin. Within Proverbs 31, your relational priorities are outlined

so that you won't be wiped out. According to God, here are the
priorities of a godly wife and mother.

God

Her relationship with God is marked by great reverence
(Song of Songs 31:30). The fear of the Lord is the beginning
of wisdom (Proverbs 9:10). Why is that true? Because if you do
not have a deep reverence for God, you will not revere his word
or his wisdom either. You will allow easier and anemic forms of
wisdom to guide your life. When we allow that to happen within our marriages and homebuilding, it is destructive. Because
this reverent woman has a healthy relationship with God, she
will not let it happen within her home. Through consistent Bible
study she has become knowledgeable enough in the Torah to
train her children (Song of Songs 31:26). The good husband of
such a woman will listen respectfully to her well-informed point
of view. He is respected at the "city gate" because her wisdom
has made him wiser (Song of Songs 31:23).

Because she knows God so deeply, she has a great trust in
his love and faithfulness (Song of Songs 31:25). From the poetry, it is obvious who is truly at the helm of this woman's life.

Her Husband

The Proverbs 31 wife understands that she is the number
two caregiver for the soul of her man. For him, the number one
"person" that should strengthen him is God. However, God engineered a wife in such a way that she could be a primary way
that he strengthens a husband. It's a big mistake to set aside
the difficult role of strengthening your husband's soul because
you think that it's God's job. It is his job, but he wants you to
help him. What a beautiful privilege, to be able to come alongside your God to be an agent in blessing your husband. A man
is greatly strengthened if in his heart he trusts that his wife is
selflessly devoted to his well-being. When a woman becomes a
wife, it radically changes her life. *"How can I strengthen my man*

today?" should be an everyday thought that beats along with her heart. The best time to be a strength to your man is when he is weak, which usually coincides with him not being a particularly good husband at the moment. My dear sisters, please reflect on what I just said. Most wives do not understand the incredible power they have to strengthen and encourage their husband. Especially when he is weary in life.

Her Children

A woman's third priority should be her children. This doesn't mean if little Johnny is throwing up in the bathroom while you're connecting with your husband that you wouldn't break away from your conversation. I probably didn't have to say that, but some people do struggle with being too rigid. Common sense says husband and wife should get up together to comfort Johnny. In my household, my wife would cuddle our little boy and I would clean up the puke. The children of this hardworking, thoughtful mother are blessed. She has provided for their most pressing needs (Song of Songs 31:13–15, 21). The husband and children of such a woman should be filled with gratitude for all that she does (Song of Songs 31:28–31). Couples without children can absorb themselves in more ministry and church building because of their streamlined schedule, while a large part of a mother's ministry is raising children to love God.

The Community

Community includes a woman's spiritual and physical families, along with her neighbors. I've seen many married couples make mistakes through one of two extremes. When children arrive, because life is so complicated and exhausting, some parents cut off priority number four. Certainly, the introduction of a child will make a huge difference in the family schedule. But it is an ungodly decision to completely hibernate away from your church and community. The other extreme is produced by guilt feelings. This happened to me when I was a young father. Conscientious Christians who long to please God often do not change their schedule enough when energy-draining children are born into the household. There were times in my kids' teenage years that I was especially absent because of ministry. Although it really wasn't because of ministry; it was because of my immature thinking. I had to realize that my first practical ministry was my wife and children. I certainly would do some things differently knowing what I know now.

Where does this relentless love warrior get her energy? (Proverbs 31:17). The Scriptures teach that when we serve with the right priorities, God will strengthen us supernaturally (Colossians 1:29; 2 Thessalonians 2:16–17; 1 Peter 4:11).

Sometimes our exhaustion is not because of how hard we work but rather due to misplaced priorities. God will sit on his hands when we're not working smart. He will allow stress and frustration into our lives, not to teach us to work less, but to convince us to work according to his wisdom. A woman who keeps her priorities straight and works hard will be blessed with energy straight from the Holy Spirit. In many cases, she will eventually be gifted with a highly motivated husband and happy children. Not having a healthy reserve of strength is not always because our priorities are messed up. There are times when the inner battle of the soul, depression, health issues, confusion, loss, tragedy, and the like can sap us of our energy. In times like these, it is crucial that married couples work as a team.

Conclusion

The Proverbs 31 woman is the builder of many rooms in the home, and her theological running mate, the Shulammite, is the builder of the bedroom. Let's remember that the *Song of Songs* is a book about healthy intimacy in all its forms, not just sexual intimacy. Understanding this helps some to not resist its message. The fact that we have an entire book in the Bible about intimacy underscores the importance of this area in our lives. To expend yourself in serving others while letting your intimacy with your spouse fall to the ground is not the picture of a prophetic marriage. The wise home builder of the *Song of Songs* has much to teach us about covenant intimacy.

In general, men and especially husbands need to give more respect to the unique wisdom that godly women possess. When I was a much younger man, I consistently gave preference to spiritual books written by male theologians. Underneath that preference was a naive disrespect for women. Even more serious was that I didn't give Kelli the respect that she deserved.

God purposely wired the female brain much differently than the male brain. God did this so that together the two genders could know and therefore image God. Whether single or married, *we need each other* to understand God accurately. As I mentioned in the introduction, Mary of Bethany understood things about Jesus that the apostles completely missed. It appears she was ahead of the men in her practical understanding of what the gospel is supposed to produce—extravagant love (Mark 14:1–9). Jesus respected her wisdom-filled response so greatly that he said that whenever and wherever the gospel is preached her story would be discussed. In the society that Mary lived in, women were not given a "seat at the table" when spiritual matters were being wrestled over. Jesus breaks that tradition in Luke 10, and even Martha is deeply bothered by the respected place that Jesus gives her sister (Luke 10:38–42). I wonder, if the apostles had imitated Jesus more in this area, would they have grasped sooner the hidden things that Mary understood?

It is more than interesting to me that the book of Proverbs, which is primarily written to men, ends with a heroic tribute to a wisdom-filled "ordinary" homemaker. Why is that? Doesn't it seem like a book written to the next generation of leaders should end with a story about a male hero? In Jewish tradition, all the men were required to memorize Proverbs 31:10–31. This was so that especially husbands would remember to give the greatest honor to the wisdom-filled love warrior they were married to. If they did, and if we do, we can know our amazing God in deeper ways.

Throughout Bible history, God has given several female theologians a seat at the table. The songs of Miriam, Deborah, Hannah, the Shulammite, and Mary the mother of Jesus are huge contributions to Scripture. Hannah's song, for example, has been used by theologians as a loose outline for 1 and 2 Samuel, and for 1 and 2 Kings. Gentlemen, if you ever wanted to get an advanced degree in family love or having compassion for the weak, you could study my wife or one of many women in the church. Since both God and Jesus gave women a seat at the table, I think we should also. Practically, this means they are respected for much more than their thoughts on the children's ministry (which is of great importance) or the church luncheon.

We should never be insecure about women wanting to "take over" or having too much power in the church. The women I know just want to help and serve. When God created Kelli to be my helper, I am convinced that the first thing on his mind was not kitchen duties and laundry. I can't tell you how many times the leaders in our church came up with a "community-changing" plan, and once we shared it with our wives it needed some significant adjustments. We were clueless about these needed changes until we talked it through with them. But far more important than plans and ministry strategies is knowing God. A woman's insight into how to help people spiritually is also of vital importance. This is where a godly woman can help the most. My favorite thing is having deep conversations with the women in my life.

Her

> Restless night after night in my bed,
>> I longed and looked for my soul's true love;
> I searched for him,
>> but I could not find him.
> I will get up now and search the city,
>> wander up and down streets and plazas;

> I will look for my soul's true love.
>> I searched for him, but I could not find him.
> The watchmen found me as they kept watch on the silent
> city.
>> "Have you seen my soul's true love?" I asked.
> Not long after I left them,
>> I found him—I found my soul's true love.
>> (Song of Songs 3:1–4 Voice)

I treasure this bit of poetry. As Song of Songs 8:6–7 describes the kind of securing love that makes a woman feel safe, the above passage reveals the kind of love that strengthens a man.

The Shulammite is desperately missing her man. Either they are not married yet or he is out of town on business. Her nightly dreams of loneliness are produced by her wholehearted love. In her dreams, she envisions finding him after a long search. When she finally discovers his whereabouts, she communicates her deep affection for him by the way she holds him. Four times in the brief poem she calls him "my soul's true love." My dear married sisters, in your heart of hearts, what human being do you love the most? What do your actions and priorities say about who your soul genuinely loves? This doesn't mean you need to love your children or grandchildren less, only possibly your husband more. How about your willingness to change and become like these two biblical wives that we've studied? Are you eager to become like, or to continue to be like, the Proverbs 31 woman and the Shulammite? Eagerly embracing God's wisdom and persisting in profuse admiration and passionate affection is how wives are called by God to strengthen their husbands.

CHAPTER 7

Intoxication

So how intoxicating is your love? What is its "alcohol content"? Solomon and his wife's love was "better than wine." In answering questions like this, I think we must be careful, because even in the Song of Songs their life together was not always intoxicating. Only sometimes; but sometimes is better than hardly ever, or never. Only in the future with God will we always be relationally intoxicated. Even the best and most experienced marriages struggle with connection. Until our intimacy is completely healed with God, we will be challenged in this area of life. My wife and I have learned to be content with this. But we can make great progress if as couples we learn to be consistently selfless, humble, and passionate with and for one another. If we put the cross at the center of our relationship in every room of the house, we can become a mystery-revealing marriage to those around us. We can enjoy more and more intoxicating moments with our lover and become an attractive advertisement for the gospel. Here is a highly instructive quote about how healthy intimacy between husband and wife can spill out into the lives of others.

We sometimes hear that Jesus doesn't ask us to like our neighbors. He only asks us to love them. And love means doing good deeds, even without any feelings of enthusiasm. That's not what draws converts to the church, though, at least not on any grand scale. Who likes to be treated that way? When it happens to us, we feel used rather than loved. We don't like it much when somebody is nice to us in order to score brownie points with God. But what happens to us inside when someone acts like they're crazy about us? How do we feel when someone is enthusiastic about being with us? How do we like it when someone likes us so much that they can't stay away, can't do enough for us, can't say enough good things about us and to us? We feel loved—that's how we feel. A passionate sexual partner certainly gives us that feeling. But true sexual healing, by spouses who are constantly passionate for each other, leads those spouses to love everyone that way. Love, when fired by sexual passion, spills over into all the other contacts that spouses have with other people. And that's the kind of love that makes the world go 'round. Dispassionate duty makes the world, and time, stand still. Passionate enthusiasm makes the world spin gloriously in its orbit.[15]

My favorite worship service is the one that I attend at our annual marriage retreat. It's not because we have orchestrated the best musicians or band to bring us to God. We usually have a skeleton crew because some talented singles and campus ministry disciples are missing. In spite of that, the singing always seems angelic, and there is an extra buzz in the fellowship. The guys are giddy and the gals are glowing. Why is that? Isn't it because we've retreated and connected? We have unplugged from "the race" and experienced some unhurried love with our spouse. We must remember that very first Sabbath was also the very first honeymoon. Maybe we should have a marriage retreat every weekend. We can't do that, but we certainly can retreat with our spouse every week. You don't have to leave home to do so, but you definitely need to be intentional. It won't happen by itself. Our hurried lifestyles blow hard against intimate connection.

So how can a husband or wife intoxicate their spouse with their love? Let's look at a few practicals.

1. Always remember the great purpose of your marriage relationship is to prophetically point to our relation-

ship with Jesus and our future with him. This should be the great "why" behind our hatred of mediocrity. Husbands, you especially should make sure that your marriage doesn't stagnate into dullness.

2. It is essential that you both learn to be experts in forgiveness. One of the greatest keys in learning how to do this is found in the sermon on the mount (Matthew 7:1–5). Learning to see yourself as just as great a sinner or an even greater one than your spouse will open the door for your heart to be empathetic and gracious. Self-righteous spouses almost always think they are better than their partner, that they are a lesser sinner. And that is the breeding ground for chronic arguments, resentment, and bitterness. When feeling angry, do not allow those feelings to control your actions. Show the actions of forgiveness, and those actions will create, by the power of the Holy Spirit, the feelings of forgiveness. Be a good slave to obedience.

3. Strive to keep your biblical priorities in their proper order. God, spouse, children, church and physical families, then community is what I have discovered the Bible teaches. To put any of these things in a different order or leave them off the list will always create problems within your marriage with God and spouse.

4. It is incorrect to teach that love is not a feeling. However, when your feelings are not in line with what love is, do not follow them. Learning to express selfless love when you're feeling selfish is one of the most fundamental things we all must do to deepen intimacy. It is key for husbands to become a safe place for their wives and for wives to be a place of strength for their husbands. Learn to be an expert at doing

the opposite of what you feel when your feelings are not in line with God's expectations. Being "not in the mood" for kitchen conversations or bedroom love is an extremely poor excuse for not serving your spouse. Why wouldn't you be willing to change anything or do something that would intoxicate your spouse with joy? As long as it is not forbidden in Scripture or by your conscience, why would you hold back? Holding back stifles intimacy, while taking God-endorsed risks can strengthen both of you. The Holy Spirit is ignited by the kind of loving that is not driven by our fickle feelings. Some protest this kind of teaching because they think if their feelings are not in line with their actions they are not being authentic. However, you don't want to be authentic to your sinful feelings, but rather to your spiritual King and the wisdom of his word. We would never think it's OK not to get up and feed a baby in the middle of the night because we are not feeling like it. Who or what do you revere the most? King Jesus or King Flesh?

5. If you are a husband, learn to think like your wife. Likewise, wives should learn to walk in their husband's shoes and think like them. As it says in 1 Corinthians 7 in the NLT, "A married man has to think about...how to please his wife" and "a married woman has to think about...how to please her husband." So listen closely, ask great questions, read good books, and study your spouse. Get off Instagram, Facebook, or the TV long enough to have some deep and healthy conversations. As a minister, I've done many funerals. And one of the most common comments I hear when someone passes away is this: "I wish I had expressed to her (or him) how I really felt more often. I wish we had spent more meaningful time together." You see,

we hold back far too often. For whatever reason, we fail to express our gratitude and love until it's too late. One of my practical goals in life is that if I suddenly lost my bride, I would not have any regrets like that at her funeral. I am trying to follow the wisdom scripture that we have studied and to express daily my love for her in a variety of ways. For many years I was a quiet husband. It was like I was allergic to meaningful conversations. Now I'm trying to make every day count and connect with Kelli, especially through focused conversations. This is the only way I can truly get to know this beautiful soul I am married to.

6. Get consistent help. Be humble enough to know that without God you will never become the kind of spouse that points prophetically to God. That challenge is far beyond human strength. Be consistent and desperate in your reliance on God. Your intimacy with your spouse will not be strengthened if your intimacy with your Father is not growing. Pray with your spouse often. Make sure that you have another couple that knows you deeply and to whom in confidence and trust you can pour out your frustrations. However, make sure they are the kind of spiritual people who will not allow you to let your frustrations run your life. Make sure they will bring you back to God and inspire you to love each other in spite of the struggle. One of the greatest signs of maturity in Christ is being able to love someone even though there is a rift between you at the moment. Have people in your life who will help you be mature like that.

7. I think it is a good practice to have a personal Bible study at least twice a week on marriage. Being a godly husband or wife is so important that I think it deserves at least that kind of attention. Along with my

daily devotional times I have practiced this for years, and it helps me not fade away and grow dull as a husband. Along with that, reading several good books each year on marriage will help you continue to be the kind of spouse that God has called you to be.

8. Work wholeheartedly to not dilute the wisdom of God in any fashion. Many times something that is "new and improved" is a good thing. But that phrase is used so often in the marketing world we assume that if something is new, that automatically means it is better. However, you cannot improve on the ancient relational wisdom in the Bible. New is never better in this area of life. God's plan for marriage and intimacy doesn't need to be updated, it needs to be understood and embraced. Be wary of relying too heavily on other good books when you have the only book from God on marriage within the Scriptures.

9. Do not multitask when you are trying to connect with your spouse. Give your wife your full attention when she is speaking. Forget about work, the bills, and the football game and listen attentively. Likewise, sisters, give your husband your full attention in the bedroom. Train your brain to be fully engaged, and your body will follow. Do not be a multitasker with your spouse.

10. Try to remember that marriage in this life is not a fairy tale. The Bible promises that "those who marry will face many troubles in this life" (1 Corinthians 7:28). The people I have counseled who are most lonely are not single people, but rather marrieds who are struggling with chronic problems in their relationship. We must be prepared for this, and those of us who are married should make sure those getting married understand this "negative" promise in the Bible.

11. Within the Bible we have the "bull's-eye" of what it means to be a husband or wife. Any of us who have been married for even a short time realizes that hitting this tiny red dot is challenging. God has some exceedingly high expectations for husbands and wives. In target-shooting competitions, there are regulations that must be followed by each competitor. A participant can't enlarge the target or get closer to it just because it's so tough to hit the bull's-eye. That would be cheating, and the person would be disqualified. Sadly, we often do that with the Bible. Because it can be overwhelming to be a scriptural husband or wife, many times, without even realizing it, we change God's expectations. We "enlarge the target" so we can feel better about ourselves. In some senses that may make life a little easier, but it always leads to dullness and mediocrity. Do not change God's requirements for marriage, but with grace and prayer intentionally strive after them. The illustration of the target is my artistic rendering of the last time I went shooting. I go about once every fifteen years, so I'm not particularly good, as the picture reveals. That day I went with three other brothers who often went shooting. You guessed it, their performance was much better than mine. Even so, I enjoyed myself a lot, mostly because no one looked down on my performance, including myself. One thing I know for sure is that if I had practiced shooting every day since then I would have progressively gotten better and therefore closer to the bull's-eye.

If we do the hard work and practice loving like Jesus daily (aiming for the bull's-eye), we will progress. It's called spiritual growth empowered by the Holy Spirit. It's crazy how in both the target-shooting world and in baseball they understand

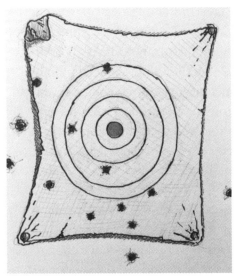

grace far better than a good number of Christians do. In the major leagues, players are paid millions of dollars and put into the Hall of Fame when they have a batting average around 300. This means they fail at bat seven out of ten times. They love to play, and we love to watch them play. It is similar in target-shooting competitions. The professionals miss the bull's-eye all the time. We can be filled with joy in our marriages even though both genders strike out or miss the bull's-eye often. But progress will be enjoyed through constant practice of the right principles. Let me ask you a question that a friend of mine, Mark Schwebach, asked of an audience that he was preaching to once. If you were offered $10,000 a month (tax free) to live out to the best of your ability what we studied in this book, would you have the motivation to do that? The goal wouldn't be perfection, but you would just have to be serious about your biblical commitments. Husbands, would you be motivated to love your wife like Jesus loves the church? Would you embrace these lofty expectations for a month, or two, or even a whole year? Would you throw away any excuses you have been making or reasons why you haven't been living this way because you would receive a big check at the end of each month? And wives, would you also be motivated to make any changes that you need to make? For money!! Something that will be completely worthless in the age to come. Shouldn't pleasing and imaging God be a far greater motivation than $10,000 a month? These are penetrating questions, and they are hard questions for me also. But they are important questions because knowledge without motivation does little good.

12. Lastly, work hard to deeply believe in your heart that King Jesus already absolutely adores you. It was Solomon's convincing admiration of his bride that finally transformed her.

> Hear this, daughter; pay close attention to what I am about to say:
>> you must forget your people and even your father's house.
> Because the king yearns for your beauty,
>> humble yourself before him, for he is now your lord.
> (Psalm 45:10–11 Voice)

Psalm 45 is a wedding song for one of Israel's kings that pointed prophetically to King Jesus' wedding. We know this to be true because part of this psalm is quoted in Hebrews chapter one. In the above verse, the bride is called to make Jesus her absolute King. Nothing is more beautiful to King Jesus than a completely surrendered bride (church). So if the King and the kingdom are not front and center in your heart, get busy repenting and watch your inner shame begin to vanish. However, there are many sold-out brides that still exist in a gloomy cloud of guilt and shame. They never feel worthy, attractive, or beautiful to their adoring spiritual Fiancé. Their overactive consciences flog them daily for their sins and shortcomings that Jesus was already flogged for. They are allergic to believing the many verses that loudly declare that King Jesus has taken away *all* their sins. I get it. It often takes a long time to believe in grace. Not so long to agree with it. But agreeing and really believing all the way down to your deepest emotions are two radically different things. The only reason that we are not worthy is because of our sins. But our sins are gone. Like, long gone. Like, as far as the east is from the west gone (Psalms 103). Like, thrown into the deepest part of the ocean gone (Micah 7:19). Fully and forever gone. Every day and always gone. You are the radiant, holy, stunning, beautiful bride right now. Believe it...enjoy it...and love him for it with all your heart and soul. I want my bride and the bride of Christ to know in their souls how breathtakingly beautiful they really are. Insecurity and shame create distance, because insecure souls often wrongly assume that God is thinking negatively about them. This, as much as any other reason, is why I wrote this book.

When the King finally returns, what are the faithful going to hear? "Well done, good and faithful servant!" (Matthew 25:21, 23). Prayerfully, we will be among them. It will be so sweet to hear the King appreciatively welcoming the genuine servants into his kingdom. It is then when we will share completely in "our master's happiness" forever. The Bible says in another verse that we will receive praise from God (1 Corinthians 4:5). Wow! God praising us! Amazing! Like the time when my son in his high school sophomore year scored 31 points in a varsity basketball game. I'm sure I was a little too boastful, because I couldn't stop talking about it. I'm still talking about it because I was so proud and excited for him! Like a proud father, God will enjoy introducing you to those who went to heaven before you. However, I think what we see will profoundly eclipse what we hear. OK, brothers, prepare yourselves, for I'm about to get a little sappy. What will we witness at the return of the King?

A couple of muscle-bound angel-ushers will open the doors. Then, like at almost every wedding I've ever officiated or attended, the trembling bridegroom will lock eyes with his radiant bride. No words will be spoken in that moment, but more will be communicated between Jesus and his bride than all the revelation already given. And our King will weep...profusely. Maybe even uncontrollably. How do you know that, Steve? How do you know what Jesus will do at that greatest of all moments? How do you know that he will break down? Because you can't love as sacrificially, patiently, deeply, and adoringly as he, and when that love finally brings forth its desired fruit, not become completely undone. You cannot pour yourself out so passionately, for so long, for this one single day, and not be filled with teary-eyed joy when that day finally arrives. And we will be awestruck, overwhelmed by the beauty of his holiness. We will finally know in our electrified souls the width, length, height, and depth of his perfect love. We will see it in his tear-filled eyes. But get this. He will be awestruck too. Like every bridegroom, he will be mesmerized, entranced, spellbound, enthralled, fascinated, captivated, and smitten to the core. He will be intoxicated by the beauty of his purified bride. The glorious princess (Psalms 45:13). The radiant wife (Ephesians 5:27). The brilliant bride shining with the glory of God (Revelation 21:11). The one who is flawless and altogether beautiful (Song of Songs 4:7). She who is as bright as the sun, majestic as the stars in procession (Song of Songs 6:10). The one who is the work of a master Artist's hands (Song of Songs 7:1; Ephesians 2:10). For the joy set before him (his wedding) he endured the cross (Song of Songs 3:11; Hebrew 12:2).

And then we will become one with our King...whatever that means! We can't imagine the unimaginable, but we know that we will be infinitely intoxicated with holy intimacy. Our souls will be completely entangled, and once again the wine of his relational glory will flow full strength in the garden of holy pleasure—it's called heaven. What was faintly pictured at that wedding in Cana (John 2:1–11) will finally be a reality forever.

Let me throw out one more thought-provoking insight. Throughout my years as a minister, I have officiated many weddings. Without exception, I have never seen an uninspired, unmotivated, or joyless bride. I've seen penniless brides, nervous brides, momentarily discouraged brides, overwhelmed brides, but I have never witnessed a gloomy, gut-it-out kind of bride. No, every woman that I ever helped marry a man was filled with lovesick enthusiasm. In fact, sometimes we got a little sick of hearing them because they would never stop talking about "the most amazing man on the face of the planet." They just could not stop sharing "the good news" about their approaching wedding day. My point should be painfully obvious. It seems to me that our future with God will be something akin to, as author Linda Dillow would put it, a never-ending "soulgasm." And that, my friends, will be much better than wine! Let me close with what I think are the three most "tattoo-worthy" scriptures in the Bible.

> As a young man marries a young woman,
> so will your builder marry *you;*
> as a bridegroom rejoices over his bride,
> so will your God rejoice over *you.*
> (Isaiah 62:5, emphasis mine)

> They will drink and roar as with wine. (Zechariah 9:15)

> *Things never discovered or heard of before, things beyond our ability to imagine*—these are the many things God has in store for all his lovers. (1 Corinthians 2:9 TPT, emphasis mine)

END NOTES

1. Christopher West, *Heaven's Song: Sexual Love as It Was Meant to Be* (Westchester, PA: Ascension Press, 2008), 2.

2. Ibid, 12–13.

3. Ellen F. Davis, *Proverbs, Ecclesiastes, and the Song of Songs* (Louisville, KY: Westminster John Knox Press, 2000), 151.

4. Ken Gire, *Incredible Moments with the Savior* (Grand Rapids, MI: Zondervan, 1990), 3.

5. Nancy Guthrie, *The Wisdom of God* (Wheaton, IL: Crossway, 2012), 254.

6. Mary Rousseau, Charles Gallagher, *Sex Is Holy* (Lockport, ME: Element, 1991), 5.

7. Robert Lewis and William Hendricks, *Rocking the Roles* (Colorado Springs, CO: Nav Press, 1991), 31.

8. Leslie Vernick, *How to Act Right When Your Spouse Acts Wrong* (New York, NY: Waterbrook, 2001), 155.

9. Carolyn Mahaney, *Feminine Appeal: Seven Virtues of a Godly Wife and Mother* (Wheaton, IL: Crossway, 2004), 27–29.

10. Phylicia Masonheimer, *Safe to Feel* (Independently published, 2019), 29.

11. Mo Isom Aiken, *Sex, Jesus, and the Conversations the Church Forgot* (Grand Rapids, MI: Baker, 2018), 12.

12. Dr. Juli Slattery, *Love, Sex and Intimacy* (Chicago, IL: Moody, 2015), 17–18.

13. Ariel Bloch and Chana Bloch, *Song of Songs: A New Translation* (London: University of California Press, 1995), 9.

14. Sam Laing, *Hot and Holy: The Five Senses of Romantic Love* (Spring, TX: Illumination Publishers, 2017), 90–91.

15. Mary Rousseau and Charles Gallagher, *Sexual Healing in Marriage* (Lockport, MA: Element, 1991), 129.

Nourish to Flourish
Ministries N2FM.org

Nourish to Flourish

- Home
- Shop
- Blog
- About
- Contact

Let go of shame. Find Joy. Know God.

Better than WINE

Steven R. Saindon

If your relationship with God were set to music, what genre of music would it be? Some grindy punk rock? A depressing country-western? Boring elevator music? Or would it be a passionate love song?

Jesus' first picture of the kingdom was at a wedding in Cana. A community celebration of two unashamed lovers whose union brilliantly revealed the lavish love God holds for his church.

Better Than Wine walks readers through this divine wedding imagery and urges us to consider what earthly marriage could be like if we only heard the love song God has always been singing to us.

For news and additional information
about Steven Saindon and the
Nourish to Flourish ministry go to
www.N2FM.org

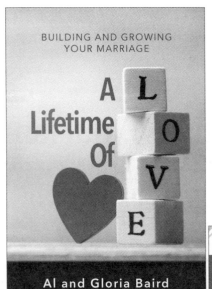

Books from
Illumination Publishers
www.ipibooks.com

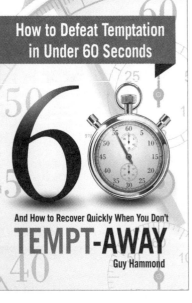

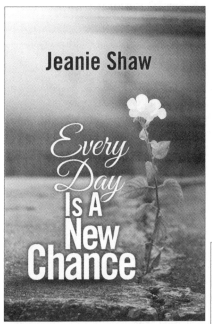

Books from

Illumination Publishers

www.ipibooks.com

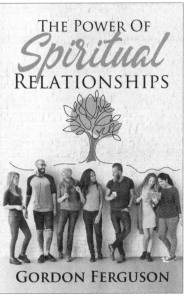

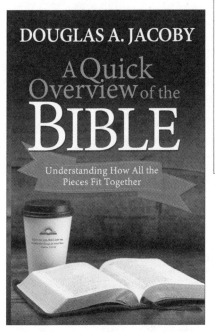

Books for Christian Growth from IP, www.ipibooks.com

Apologetics

Compelling Evidence for God and the Bible—Truth in an Age of Doubt, by Douglas Jacoby.
Field Manual for Christian Apologetics, by John M. Oakes.
Is There A God—Questions and Answers about Science and the Bible, by John M. Oakes.
Mormonism—What Do the Evidence and Testimony Reveal?, by John M. Oakes.
Reasons For Belief–A Handbook of Christian Evidence, by John M. Oakes.
That You May Believe—Reflections on Science and Jesus, by John Oakes/David Eastman.
The Resurrection: A Historical Analysis, by C. Foster Stanback.
When God Is Silent—The Problem of Human Suffering, by Douglas Jacoby.

Bible Basics

A Disciple's Handbook—Third Edition, Tom A. Jones, Editor.
A Quick Overview of the Bible, by Douglas Jacoby.
Be Still, My Soul—A Practical Guide to a Deeper Relationship with God, by Sam Laing.
From Shadow to Reality—Relationship of the Old & New Testament, by John M. Oakes.
Deep Convictions—13 Week Study Guide, by Tom A. Jones.
Getting the Most from the Bible, Second Edition, by G. Steve Kinnard.
Letters to New Disciples—Practical Advice for New Followers of Jesus, by Tom A. Jones.
The Baptized Life—The Lifelong Meaning of Immersion into Christ, by Tom A. Jones.
The Lion Never Sleeps—Preparing Those You Love for Satans Attacks, by Mike Taliaferro.
The New Christian's Field Guide, Joseph Dindinger, Editor.
Thirty Days at the Foot of the Cross, Tom and Sheila Jones, Editors.

Christian Living

According to Your Faith—The Awesome Power of Belief in God, by Richard Alawaye.
But What About Your Anger—A Biblical Guide to Managing Your Anger, by Lee Boger.
Caring Beyond the Margins—Understanding Homosexuality, by Guy Hammond.
Golden Rule Membership—What God Expects of Every Disciple, by John M. Oakes.
How to Defeat Temptation in Under 60 Seconds, by Guy Hammond.
Jesus and the Poor—Embracing the Ministry of Jesus, by G. Steve Kinnard.
How to Be a Missionary in Your Hometown, by Joel Nagel.
Like a Tree Planted by Streams of Water—Personal Spiritual Growth, G. Steve Kinnard.
Love One Another—Importance & Power of Christian Relationships, by Gordon Ferguson.
One Another—Transformational Relationships, by Tom A. Jones and Steve Brown.
Prepared to Answer—Restoring Truth in An Age of Relativism, by Gordon Ferguson.
Repentance—A Cosmic Shift of Mind & Heart, by Edward J. Anton.
Strong in the Grace—Reclaiming the Heart of the Gospel, by Tom A. Jones.
The Guilty Soul's Guide to Grace—Freedom in Christ, by Sam Laing.
The Killer Within, by Michael Taliaferro.
*The One Another Handbook—Toney C. Mulhollan, Editor.
The Power of Discipling, by Gordon Ferguson.
The Prideful Soul's Guide to Humility, by Tom A. Jones and Michael Fontenot.
The Sacred Journey—Finding God in Caregiving, by Jeanie Shaw and Friends.
The Way of the Heart—Spiritual Living in a Legalistic World, by G. Steve Kinnard.
The Way of the Heart of Jesus—Prayer, Fasting, Bible Study, by G. Steve Kinnard.
Till the Nets Are Full—An Evangelism Handbook for the 21st Century, by Douglas Jacoby.
Walking the Way of the Heart—Lessons for Spiritual Living, by G. Steve Kinnard.
Values and Habits of Spiritual Growth, by Bryan Gray.

Deeper Study

A Women's Ministry Handbook, by Jennifer Lambert and Kay McKean.

After The Storm—Hope & Healing From Ezra—Nehemiah, by Rolan Dia Monje.

Aliens and Strangers—The Life and Letters of Peter, by Brett Kreider.

Crossing the Line: Culture, Race, and Kingdom, by Michael Burns.

Daniel—Prophet to the Nations, by John M. Oakes.

Exodus—Making Israel's Journey Your Own, by Rolan Dia Monje.

Exodus—Night of Redemption, by Douglas Jacoby.

Finish Strong—The Message of Haggai, Zechariah, and Malachi, by Rolan Dia Monje.

Free Your Mind—40 Days to Greater Peace, Hope, and Joy, by Sam Laing.

God, Are We Good, Can I Know for Sure, by Gordon Ferguson.

In Remembrance of Me—Understanding the Lord's Supper, by Andrew C. Fleming.

In the Middle of It!—Tools to Help Preteen and Young Teens, by Jeff Rorabaugh.

Into the Psalms—Verses for the Heart, Music for the Soul, by Rolan Dia Monje.

King Jesus—A Survey of the Life of Jesus the Messiah, by G. Steve Kinnard.

Jesus Unequaled—An Exposition of Colossians, by G. Steve Kinnard.

Mornings in Matthew, by Tammy Fleming.

Passport to the Land of Enough—Revised Edition, by Joel Nagel.

Prophets I—The Voices of Yahweh, by G. Steve Kinnard.

Prophets II—The Prophets of the Assyrian Period, by G. Steve Kinnard.

Prophets III—The Prophets of the Babylonian and Persion Periods, by G. Steve Kinnard.

Return to Sender—When There's Nowhere Left to God but Home, by Guy Hammond.

Romans—The Heart Set Free, by Gordon Ferguson.

Revelation Revealed—Keys to Unlocking the Mysteries of Revelation, by Gordon Ferguson.

Spiritual Leadership for Women, Jeanie Shaw, Editor.

Spiritual Transformation, by Cresenda Jones.

The Call of the Wise—An Introduction and Index of Proverbs, by G. Steve Kinnard.

The Cross of the Savior—From the Perspective of Jesus..., by Mark Templer.

The Final Act—A Biblical Look at End-Time Prophecy, by G. Steve Kinnard.

The Gospel of Matthew—The Crowning of the King, by G. Steve Kinnard.

The Letters of James, Peter, John, Jude—Life to the Full, by Douglas Jacoby.

The Lion Has Roared—An Exposition of Amos, by Douglas Jacoby.

The Seven People Who Help You to Heaven, by Sam Laing.

The Spirit—Presense & Power, Sense & Nonsense, by Douglas Jacoby.

Thrive—Using Psalms to Help You Flourish, by Douglas Jacoby.

What Happens After We Die?, by Douglas Jacoby.

World Changers—The History of the Church in the Book of Acts, by Gordon Ferguson.

Marriage and Family

A Lifetime of Love—Building and Growing Your Marriage, by Al and Gloria Baird.

Building Emotional Intimacy in Your Marriage, by Jeff and Florence Schachinger.

Hot and Holy—God's Plan for Exciting Sexual Intimacy in Marriage, by Sam Laing.

Faith and Finances, by Patrick Blair.

Friends & Lovers—Marriage as God Designed It, by Sam and Geri Laing.

Mighty Man of God—A Return to the Glory of Manhood, by Sam Laing.

Pure the Journey—A Radical Journey to a Pure Heart, by David and Robin Weidner.

Raising Awesome Kids—Being the Great Influence in Your Kids' Lives by Sam and Geri Laing.

Principle-Centered Parenting, by Douglas and Vicki Jacoby.

The Essential 8 Principles of a Growing Christian Marriage, by Sam and Geri Laing.

The Essential 8 Principles of a Strong Family, by Sam and Geri Laing.

The Essential 8 Principles of Godly Parenting, by Sam and Geri Laing.

Warrior—A Call to Every Man Everywhere, by Sam Laing.

For additional books go to
www.ipibooks.com